In the
18th-Century Style

In the 18th-Century Style

Building Furniture Inspired by the Classical Tradition

The Taunton Press

The Taunton Press
Inspiration for hands-on living™

The Taunton Press, Inc., 63 South Main Street, PO Box 5506, Newtown, CT 06470-5506

e-mail: tp@taunton.com

Distributed by Publishers Group West

Jacket/Cover design: Susan Fazekas

Interior design: Susan Fazekas

Layout: Carol Petro

Front Cover Photographers: Zachary Gaulkin, © The Taunton Press, Inc. (large); Jonathan Binzen, © The Taunton Press, Inc. (inset, left); © Joel Breger & Associates (inset center); Dennis Preston, © The Taunton Press, Inc. (inset right)

Back Cover Photographers: © Paul Zenaty (bottom); Zachary Gaulkin, © The Taunton Press, Inc. (inset left); © Lance Patterson (inset center); Michael Pekovich, © The Taunton Press, Inc. (inset right)

Spine Photographer: © Lance Patterson

Library of Congress Cataloging-in-Publication Data
In the 18th century style: building furniture inspired by the classical
    tradition/the editors of Fine woodworking.
        p. cm.
    Includes index.
    ISBN 1-56158-397-9
    1. Furniture making--Amateurs' manuals. 2. Furniture--United
States--History--18th century.   I. Fine woodworking.
    TT195.I47 2002
    681.1'04--dc21

                            2002009056

Printed in the United States of America

10 9 8 7 6 5 4 3 2 1

The following manufacturers/names appearing in *In the 18th-Century Style* are trademarks: 3M's Spray Mount, Delta, Dremel, Eberle, Godiva, Minwax, Mylar, Olson, Plexiglas, Scotch-Brite, Sears.

■ Working wood is inherently dangerous. Using hand or power tools improperly or ignoring safety practices can lead to permanent injury or even death. Don't try to perform operations you learn about here (or elsewhere) unless you're certain they are safe for you. If something about an operation doesn't feel right, don't do it. Look for another way. We want you to enjoy the craft, so please keep safety foremost in your mind whenever you're in the shop.

Special thanks to the authors, editors, art directors, copy editors, and other staff members of *Fine Woodworking* and *Home Furniture* who contributed to the development of the articles in this book.

CONTENTS

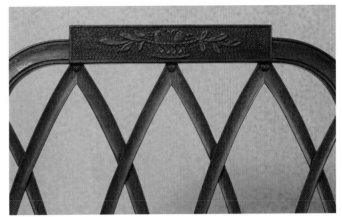

Why do the world's woodworkers return again and again to the classic furniture styles of the 18th century? Time is typically not kind to decorative styles, especially 300 years of changing fad and fashion. However, furniture from the Colonial period remains classic because it exhibits exquisite proportion, unforgettable form, and beautiful detail. The period actually covers several distinct styles but it represents probably the most extraordinary 100 years of furniture design.

In this most incredible century, we awoke from the raw utility of pilgrim plank furniture and did not tire creatively until we had produced shapely and eloquent styles remembered now as William and Mary, Queen Anne, Chippendale, Sheraton, Federal, and Hepplewhite. The furniture was delicate, graceful, and light on its feet. The styles all found new ways to mimic classic sensuous forms such as that of the vase, the S-shaped cyma curve, and the slipper foot. It flowed from top to bottom and back up in a way that wood had never been manipulated. It represented an entire world discovering other parts of itself: from Chinese-influenced ball-and-claw feet to the use of the great mahogany trees from the Caribbean.

The period's cabinetmakers worked with relatively simple tools that still represent purity to a large and dedicated group of today's woodworkers. The drawknives, chisels, saws, and marking tools used today differ little from those used by 18th-century workers who had no electricity.

But the attraction of this classic furniture is its timeless beauty. An 18th-century highboy or secretary still represents the highest form of woodworking achievement to most of us who practice the craft. It often represents the visible proof that one has mastered most facets of woodworking: joinery, carving, turning, inlay, marquetry, and finishing.

The Taunton Press editors of this book looked to the pages of *Fine Woodworking* and *Home Furniture* magazines to share with you the period's luxurious beauty. Part One of the book covers the historical background of the century's styles; Part Two contains techniques and projects to help you make this wonderful furniture yourself; Part Three includes inspiring examples made by today's best woodworking artisans. Together the sections represent a unique guide to the world's most classic furniture.

—Tim Schreiner, publisher of *Fine Woodworking* and former editor of *Home Furniture*

Style & Design

While other furniture styles have come and gone, 18th-century furniture remains popular. Its elegant lines, sensuous curves, and sense of proportion give it a timeless quality. The very names—Queen Anne, Chippendale, Hepplewhite, Sheraton—have become synonymous with classic furniture design.

In this section, you'll learn about some of the most famous makers of 18th-century furniture and their hallmark designs. And you'll learn about mahogany: Prized for its beauty, durability, and utilitarian attributes, it was the ideal wood for 18th-century styles.

JENNIFER A. PERRY

Federal Furniture Was Revolutionary

At the Smithsonian Institution, in Washington, D.C, you can see the portable desk on which Thomas Jefferson wrote the Declaration of Independence. The desk is simple. Its only decoration is a light string inlay made of satinwood. Jefferson said the desk "is plain, neat, convenient, and...yet displays itself sufficiently." Symbolic of the country's birth, the desk also represents a new furniture style that, like Jefferson's principles, became known for its elegant simplicity and efficiency.

The desk is thought to be one of the first pieces of American Federal furniture—the style that became fashionable during the latter years of the American Revolution and remained popular through the first quarter of the 19th century.

The sleek lines, carefully chosen woods, and smooth surfaces of American Federal furniture link it aesthetically with much of today's studio furniture. And like many of today's furniture makers, Federal cabinetmakers prided themselves on their craftsmanship. But the reasons behind the creation and popularity of Federal furniture were complex and unique. Its designs and motifs proclaimed loudly and clearly that America was a new and independent nation with aspirations no less lofty than those of the ancient Greeks and Romans.

Cabinetmakers made a distinctively American statement: We are one people who will strive to do things righteously, but we will do things our way.

CUTTING-EDGE CLASSICAL

Two hundred years can add a lot of patina to a piece of furniture, and it can also add to our sense of its formality, its seriousness. But late in the 18th century, when the Federal style came into its own, it was, primarily, the latest thing in home decorating. We like to think of the men who founded this country as being beyond reproach, but they were not beyond the whims of fashion. After the discovery of the ruins of Pompeii in the middle of the 18th century, all things classical were in vogue. The new nation of America grabbed onto classicism like a teenager going after a latest fad. Paintings from the time of the Revolution often depicted George Washington in a toga, and he was frequently described as a mythical figure.

Before the days of home-decorating magazines, American cabinetmakers looked to England for inspiration. Late in the 18th century, two English design books that promoted neoclassical style were published. George Hepplewhite's *Cabinet-Maker and*

A NEW STYLE FOR A NEW NATION. As America declared its independence, Federal furniture became the rage. Bright veneers and inlays, classical decorations, and lighter, linear forms replaced the ornate curved and carved surfaces of the Chippendale and Queen Anne styles.

ICONS FROM GREECE AND ROME. The eagle, a Roman symbol of power, became emblematic for America, and adorned Federal furniture in inlays, carvings, even drawer pulls (above). The 13 stars shown represent the original colonies. Left, a goddess in a chariot adorns a mirror panel. A decorative column is inlaid on a desk front (facing page). A chair splat is carved with an urn (bottom).

Upholsterer's Guide and Thomas Sheraton's *The Cabinet-Maker and Upholsterer's Drawing Book* concentrated on the use of classical form and ornament in furniture design.

Classical figures—gods and goddesses—and classical accoutrements like swags, urns, medallions, and columns were all part of the neoclassical design vocabulary, and Americans made them their own. Bell-flowers were inlaid onto drawers, swags were tacked onto chair rails, and urns were carved onto chair backs.

Americans enhanced their borrowed repertoire of classical designs with a significant addition of their own: the eagle. Perhaps the most popular image during the Federal era, the eagle was a symbol of Roman power and had been made America's official mascot in 1782. It became the identifying American image, and it was seen everywhere—from finials to drawer pulls.

LINE, INLAY, AND COLOR

There was more to the Federal style than
adding an inlaid eagle or a carved urn here
and there. In some senses, the Federal style
was a reaction to the styles that came before
it. If it can be said that the Queen Anne
and Chippendale styles were based on
curves, Federal was based on line.

Almost without exception, Federal furniture has a delicate, linear, almost wispy
appearance. Chair and table legs are thin
and straight, and many chairs have no
stretchers between their legs. The furniture
often seems to be standing on tiptoes.
Upholstery is taut and flat, and chair seats
are usually rectilinear.

Cabriole legs, a stylistic given during the
Queen Anne and Chippendale eras, gave way
to round or square tapered legs. The Queen
Anne slipper foot and the Chippendale ball-
and-claw foot were left behind in favor of
simpler square or turned feet.

This is not to say that Federal furniture
is all straight lines and rectilinear shapes.
Curves abound on Federal furniture, but
they are, for the most part, linear rather
than compound: Imagine a linear curve as a
cylinder, curving in only one direction, and
a compound curve as a sphere, which curves
in several directions.

The Federal emphasis on line was not
limited to form and mass; it was also
manifested in decoration, specifically inlay.
Federal case pieces look as if they are
composed of geometric puzzle pieces, with
ovals, rectangles, and circles fit together.

Whereas the Queen Anne and Chippendale styles were known for carved ornamentation, Federal furniture focused on
smooth surface decoration. Carving certainly appeared on Federal pieces, especially
on chair splats and legs, but it was carving
as decoration rather than the deep, sculp-
tural carving typical of Chippendale furniture.

Federal cabinetmakers favored mahogany
as a primary wood, but they also began
using a variety of bright, light-colored

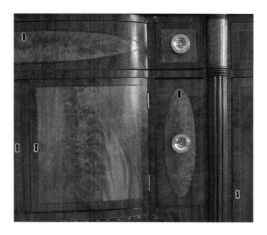

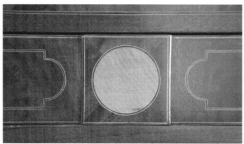

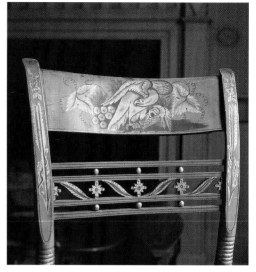

BEYOND BASIC BROWN WOOD FURNITURE.
Geometric shapes in light-colored woods,
line inlays, and formal, painted furniture, like
this New York chair with a decorative eagle
(top right), are hallmarks of Federal furniture.

woods for highlights and veneers, woods
like maple, satinwood, boxwood, holly, rosewood, and birch.

Inlaid pieces often had subtle shading,
achieved by putting the pieces into hot sand
which burned or charred the wood. The
variety of light and dark color combina-
tions became a hallmark of Federal furniture. Even after 200 years, the bright-
colored woods, varnished or shellacked,
almost shimmer as light reflects off their
polished surfaces.

NEW FURNITURE FORMS

Years ago, before VCRs, before the term
"couch potato" was invented, no one had
entertainment centers in their homes.
Lifestyle changes brought about new furniture forms. Similarly, in the Federal period,
new furniture forms came about in response
to changes in Americans' pocketbooks,
expectations, and lifestyles.

The most significant new form in the
Federal period was the sideboard (see photo
on p. 7). At the end of the 18th century,
rooms in Federal homes became more spe-
cialized, so furniture was created to fit
rooms' new functions. As Americans began
to differentiate between a sitting room and
a dining room, sideboards were designed so

A QUANTUM LEAP FROM CABRIOLE LEGS WITH BALL-AND-CLAW-FEET. In the left photo, simple, straight, bracket feet support a Federal chest. Above, a card table and a candlestand look as if they stand on tiptoes.

that meals could be served in the new room set aside for that specific purpose.

The introduction of tambour and cylinder desks reflected the changing roles of men and women in the Federal period. Sometimes known as ladies' desks, they are thought to have been used more by women than men and may have been created to meet an increased interest in women's learning. These desks were smaller than the large desks and secretaries of the past, indicating they were most likely used less for business and more for pleasure.

CLASSIC LINES, CLASSICAL MOTIFS. The supporting columns and the carved eagle finial on this looking glass are among the defining elements of Federal furniture.

Worktables with a cloth or wooden drawer to hold a woman's needlework were a sign of social status and disposable income. Some worktables included a writing surface inside a top drawer, another sign of women's educational accomplishments.

Banjo wall clocks, patented by Simon Willard of Massachusetts in 1802, sold for about two-thirds the price of an average tall case clock and permitted many Americans the luxury of owning a highly desirable decorative object. They featured geometric shapes, eagles, and other patriotic emblems, gold leaf and painting on glass, and are considered a pinnacle of neoclassical design.

Card tables were made before the Federal period, but it was during this time that their manufacture proliferated. Card playing was a popular Federal-era pastime, but more than that, lightweight, portable, and often highly embellished card tables were used as decorative elements in Federal households. Often made in pairs, Federal card tables were placed under windows or mirrors to give a room the desired symmetrical appearance.

A variety of new chair styles with classical and patriotic motifs appeared in the Federal period. Most notable is the lolling chair, now usually called a Martha Washington chair. It is a unique American Federal form with a high upholstered back and upholstered seat. Unlike the Chippendale wing chair, its arms are open and unupholstered. The open arms give the chair a light look, and they suggest a casual posture, perhaps an allusion to a lifestyle that made time for relaxation and leisure.

No furniture is created in a vacuum. Federal furniture drew on motifs from ancient Greece and Rome and used them in a lighter, delicate style that fit the fashionable impulses of a new country. Many of the furniture forms developed during the Federal period are still being made today, and it is hard to deny Federal's stylistic influence on much of today's studio furniture.

A GEOMETRIC JIGSAW PUZZLE. Book-matched mahogany drawer fronts, line inlays, and veneered ovals add to the visual complexity of the straight lines of this secretary.

EMYL JENKINS

Queen Anne

You think we're living in a fast-paced world? Picture this. It's 1680. You've just finished eating your dinner off a wooden plate in a stone manor house somewhere in South Yorkshire. You lean back in your wretchedly uncomfortable, deeply carved, high-backed, plank-seated, oak wainscot chair. You prop your feet up on a huge, rectangular table supported by massive bulbous legs and held together by strong box stretchers. Rip Van Winkle-style, you doze off.

You awaken 40 years later in 1720. In your brick house you are slumped over in a much slimmer Queen Anne walnut chair with a scooped out, vase-shaped backsplat, gracefully curved cabriole legs, rounded arms, and a padded, upholstered seat. Your feet have slipped off the all-purpose refectory table, a bulky, 9-ft. immovable monster. In its place stands an easily transportable, fold-over card table with a veneered apron and shell-carved cabriole legs.

Furniture underwent dramatic changes in a matter of a handful of years at the beginning of the 18th century. During Queen Anne's reign (1702–1714), primarily utilitarian Jacobean furniture became transformed into an art form. The new style changed furniture making both aesthetically and structurally. That which was austere became graceful; the clunky emerged elegant; and linear turned curvaceous. Furniture makers came up with new construction methods and new furniture forms.

EASTERN INFLUENCE ON WESTERN FURNITURE

Before 1700, with the exception of elite centers of court life in Europe, most people were living in the shadow of the Middle Ages. What we think of as civilized life was just emerging from medieval times. Forks had been in use, even among European royalty, for only 100 years. Homes were still crudely built for the most part, and jousting was still commonplace in the countryside.

A combination of unprecedented strides in craftsmanship and commerce brought European furniture out of its almost totally utilitarian function into the status of an art form. Half a world away from an awakening Europe, the Chinese were making highly refined, curvaceous, and exquisitely lacquered furniture—and had been for 2,100 years. In the 16th and 17th centuries, adventuresome European explorers—first the Portuguese, then the Dutch and the English—brought the more advanced Asian furniture shapes and lines to their lands. When those designs were adapted to suit

THE ROYAL CURVES. The S curve typical of the period appears on this Queen Anne highboy in the cabriole legs, molding, bonnet-top pediment, and even on drawer pulls.

THE GRACE OF A FLOWING LINE. The distinguishing element of Queen Anne chairs is the S curve on cabriole legs, vase-shaped backsplat, and yoked crest rail.

the European home, a new level of style and comfort became part of Western culture and daily life. Equally important, a full-blown and bustling new furniture-making industry was born.

Dutch merchants began the trend by sending whole shiploads of cabinets, desks, and chests to China for lacquering. When they were returned to Holland, these lustrously decorated pieces were sold for a handsome profit. Dutch furniture makers caught on quickly. By the late 1600s they began incorporating the more graceful Chinese elements—primarily the curved crest and a backsplat slightly spooned to follow the human form—in their European designs. This new style spread to England when the Netherlands' William of Orange was invited to succeed James II on the English throne in 1688.

THE IRRESISTIBLE CURVE

English furniture makers quickly seized the opportunity. The emerging merchant class had money to spend and demanded luxury at home. The cry was for furniture that looked totally different from the angular oak furniture they already had. In a word, they wanted curves—curves made of walnut and mahogany. So curves popped up everywhere. In addition to cabriole legs and rounded backsplats, there were yoke-shaped crest rails, bow-fronted hanging cupboards, rounded turrets on tables to hold candlesticks, and gracefully arched pediments on secretaries and bookcases. English craftsmen experimented and chiseled out softer, curving lines. They also created a whole new vocabulary of furniture forms.

FURNITURE FOR THE GOOD LIFE

The all-purpose storage chest with a lift-up top evolved into the much-improved, and streamlined, chest of drawers.

Settles, those wooden benches from the Middle Ages that served for sitting and sleeping, with a storage section beneath, became sofas with stuffed seats and backs made solely for sitting.

The oversized table, which was once used for eating, business, and occasionally sleeping, shrank. Furthermore, tables were made for specific purposes: writing, games, grooming, and just plain ornamentation.

The middle class wanted small mirrors in carved frames and freestanding candlestands. Even the cupboard, that utilitarian piece originally intended for keeping a family's meager bed linen and clothing or food, was redesigned to show off treasured pewter plates, brass candlesticks—and, in the well-to-do home, sterling silver salt trenchers and Chinese export china.

Hand in hand, life and furniture rapidly changed. The early 18th century was a relatively peaceful time politically and socially when compared to the warring eras that sandwiched it. Calm and assurance were reflected in the strong, serene lines of the furniture.

A CURVACEOUS TABLE. This Queen Anne tea table has C-scroll bracketed cabriole legs, cusps on the corners, a scalloped apron, and convex curves on the tray molding.

THE IMPORTANCE OF FORM AND FUNCTION

Furniture made between 1702 (when Queen Anne ascended the throne) and 1760 (by which time the Chippendale style had secured a stronghold) can withstand even the closest scrutiny. It was beautifully proportioned, finely crafted, and so much more comfortable than that which had come before.

Still, like the nearly indestructible, angular Jacobean furniture that preceded it, Queen Anne furniture was soundly constructed, well-joined, and sturdy. Initially, however, the introduction of the curvaceous, feminine cabriole leg posed some problems. When furniture makers tried to keep the ample width of the seat and the height of the high-backed wainscot chair, the relatively slender supporting cabriole legs proved too spindly and weak. The solution was to do what chairmakers had always done: insert stretchers between the legs.

PRIOR TO THE QUEEN. The Jacobean furniture that preceded Queen Anne style in most homes was angular, heavy, and bulky.

A WRITING STYLE ALL ITS OWN. Writing desks had been boxes nailed to legs before the advent of the Queen Anne desk.

A HUMBLE QUEEN. Although Queen Anne is seen as ornate today, it was spare compared to the heavily carved Jacobean period that preceded it and the rococo Chippendale style that followed it.

Stretchers provided the needed strength, but they broke the graceful, curved lines of the chair legs. Around 1720, there was a breakthrough. Chairmakers realized that by lowering the chair back a little, fleshing out the legs, and adding hidden corner braces, the stretcher could be omitted.

LEG STRUCTURE EVOLVES WITH FUNCTION

The strong joinery on otherwise delicate-looking legs proved sturdy enough for the weight of the human body as well as the heft of tables, desks, and lowboy chests. But large, heavy chests of drawers presented more difficult problems. Before 1700, chests of drawers were available in two styles: the typical, four-drawer, low chest with chunky, bun feet; and a taller variety with the four drawers stacked atop a leggy stand fitted with an additional drawer.

As fashion moved to the Queen Anne style, the low chests remained basically the same, but the feet were replaced with either sturdy bracket feet or curved feet (which were called "ogee feet"). The taller chests on stands had been supported by hefty turned legs—often four legs across the front and two in back—linked by beefy stretchers.

By 1720, however, nothing would do but stretcherless, and less sturdy, cabriole legs. Even though corner blocks were used around the interior of the stand frame, the cabriole legs often split and even gave way under too much weight. Most furniture makers soon abandoned this very attractive, but not too practical, Queen Anne chest for the style of large chest that evolved next, the Chippendale, bracket-footed chest on chest.

On smaller pieces, such as the Queen Anne writing desk, the cabriole legs proved to be perfect. In the 17th century, the first writing desks had been little more than a box nailed onto four legs. From this humble

EARLY ARRIVAL OF THE QUEEN. William and Mary style was found only in rich homes. This transitional piece has elements of Queen Anne, along with the trumpet-turned legs and thick stretchers of William and Mary.

beginning came a perennially popular furniture form: the slanted, pull-down writing surface made graceful and appealing by the presence of shapely legs. Measuring no more than 3 ft. across, this serviceable piece still remains ideal today for use in any number of rooms in smaller homes.

THE QUEEN OF DESIGN IN AMERICA

Americans embraced graceful Queen Anne furniture as soon as they discovered it, or approximately two decades after the style emerged in England. This popularity was helped by the fact that colonists were beginning to prosper by the 1720s, and an influx of English craftsmen brought knowledge of the new fashion to these shores. Queen Anne furniture also remained popular in America longer than in England because it took years for the style to filter out to the majority of the population in the rural countryside. Americans didn't even object to the furniture style being named for a British monarch.

Some 150 years later, around 1900, when reproductions of earlier styles reemerged as fashionable, the dignified but romantic Queen Anne style once again became popular—but with notable differences. Manufacturing companies, no longer

■ EVOLUTION OF THE QUEEN ANNE CHAIR

In the 17th century, wainscot chairs had high-paneled backs and plank seats attached to simple foursquare frames.

European sea traders brought ideas back from China, where chairs had long been designed with curves in stiles, crest rails, and backsplats.

Early Queen Anne chairs retained the turned legs and bulbous stretchers of earlier chairs but added curves on the backs.

limited by the construction problems that had challenged 18th-century craftsmen, used modern methods and bent some tenets of the style to capture the revival look. They created Queen Anne-style sideboards (although there had not been such a form until approximately the coming of the Hepplewhite period in 1780), coffee tables (a distinctly 20th-century form), and Victrolas with cabriole legs. These "modern" pieces became as essential to the stylish 1920s house as the Queen Anne card table had been in the 1720s.

In their favor was the very same characteristic that made Queen Anne pieces so appealing from the beginning—the curves. One cabriole-legged piece placed in a room of angular and straight-legged furniture softens the look, adds interest to the decor, and becomes an immediate focal point.

The graceful curve is ever-appealing, no matter what the year. That's why the Chinese embraced the curving line in furniture design 20 centuries ago. That's why westerners so quickly fell in love with the look 300 years ago. It also is the reason why graceful and aesthetically pleasing Queen Anne furniture continues to reign as the queen of furniture design.

The elimination of stretchers was a breakthrough made possible by adding corner blocks and beefing up the legs.

A curved seat rail made it necessary for some early chairmakers to return to using stretchers as a major support element.

The culmination of Queen Anne chair design: No stretchers block the lower half, and all surfaces have graceful curves.

WALTER RAYNES

Choosing Brass Hardware for Period Furniture

Let's suppose you're about to build a piece of traditional American furniture—something like that chest of drawers you saw in a museum. You probably will spend some time finding the right boards and figuring out how to reproduce the joinery faithfully. But have you forgotten something? Ah, yes, the hardware. If you think that picking the hardware is as simple as opening a mail-order catalog, you may want to think again.

Brass hardware, especially visible and decorative items like drawer pulls and escutcheons, has a tremendous effect on the look of period furniture. When these pieces were built originally, hardware selection was not

REPRODUCTIONS CAN CAPTURE ORIGINAL DETAILS. This hand-carved die and the Hepplewhite-style backplate made from it by Horton Brasses show the level of detail possible in brass reproduction hardware.

left to chance any more than decisions on joinery or veneers. The best pieces of period furniture were designed so that all the details worked together.

In a great many pieces of Federal style furniture, for example, geometric shapes and inlays have their counterpart in the brass ovals used for the drawer pulls. In more ornate pieces, like some Chippendale highboys, the hardware style is completely different. There, you may find the rococo flourishes of the brasses mirrored in the woodworking itself.

Before opening the hardware catalogs and placing your order, examine several original hardware examples carefully. Look at all the different elements and you will probably notice the integration of proportion, decoration, and hardware. The chart on p. 24 illustrates relationships between furniture styles and hardware for some of the most recognizable periods of traditional American furniture.

Taking the time to look at the subtle details of pieces from these periods will help guide you in your search for the right hardware for your reproduction furniture. Knowing something about how the hardware is made also is a benefit, since manufacturing methods often determine how authentic a reproduction looks. Brass hardware today is available in many styles and is made in different ways. And, of course, the better reproductions will cost more, perhaps twice as much as their standard-quality equivalents.

HOW PERIOD REPRODUCTIONS ARE MADE

Most brass hardware today is die-cast, stamped, or cut from large sheets. Some of it may even be made from brass-plated steel or brass-plated zinc alloys. Modern manufacturing methods involve little handwork, and, therefore, can churn out large quantities of identical and relatively inexpensive pieces. Most early brass hardware, however, was anything but uniform, and if

Style	Common Hardware	How It Was Made
William and Mary (1680–1730) 	Teardrop or pear-shaped pulls, backed by rosettes, loosely echo the shapes of turned legs popular during the period. Rosettes in their simplest form were circular; more elaborate rosettes had cast or stamped decoration.	Cast, hand-chased
Queen Anne (1720–1760) 	Bails, or handles, on drawer pulls are used with decorated backplates. Later styles used post-and-nut mountings instead of wire. Bails often adopted the ogee curves found in the legs and moldings of the period.	Cast, hand-chased
Chippendale (1750–1790) 	Brass hardware evolved into more elaborate rococo patterns in keeping with the furniture itself. Toward the end of the period, cast "bat wing" backplates were sometimes replaced by simple button-and-bail pulls.	Cast
Hepplewhite (1790–1810) 	A sharp, stylistic shift occurred due to changing manufacturing methods. Oval pulls often had elaborate decoration, such as the eagle motif, a popular symbol reflecting the pride of a new nation. The oval shape of the backplates mirrors the elliptical inlays and other geometric patterns found in the furniture.	Cast and stamped elements
Sheraton (1800–1820)	Brass knobs, similar in style and decoration to the Hepplewhite period, gained wide popularity. The decoration of the knobs mirrors carved rosettes found in furniture that reflected the designs of Thomas Sheraton.	Cast and stamped elements

REPRODUCTIONS CAN BE EXPENSIVE.
A Ball and Ball employee files a Chippendale escutcheon by hand. This time-consuming process is necessary for a faithful reproduction.

POURING BRASS IS HARD WORK. Molten brass, heated to 2,100°F, is poured into sand molds at Horton Brasses. The sand molds are destroyed after every pour.

price is no object, you usually can find reproduction hardware that is made exactly as it was originally.

Before 1750, most brass hardware was cast in sand molds. To sand-cast a part, a pattern of the part is pressed into a sand mold. The pattern is removed, and molten brass is poured into the mold, cooling in the shape of the pattern. Sand-casting is still practiced today, and is generally considered the best process for hardware on reproductions of that era because of the subtle but noticeable differences it imparts to the hardware. For example, the backplates of cast drawer pulls, escutcheons, and rosettes were filed by hand to produce a beveled edge. Much of this early hardware was "chased," a process in which decoration is hammered into the brass by hand. Also,

slight surface imperfections and undulations resulting from the casting process are apparent, even at a distance. The same is true for other cast parts, such as the bails, or handles, on drawer pulls. Many of the cheaper reproductions, by comparison, appear absolutely flat and uniform, lacking the subtle variations of sand-cast parts.

The availability of thin sheet brass after 1750 allowed decoration to be stamped into the metal by machine. This new technology led, during the Federal era in the late 1700s, to oval backplates often stamped with intricate designs. The Hepplewhite style ovals show incredible detail. Efforts to re-create these designs have led to some high-quality dies. Some of the less expensive reproductions, however, have been simplified for ease of production (although the process remains basically the same). If a reproduction oval lacks the detail or crispness of an original, the hardware will look out of place.

One difficulty in searching for period brasses is that not all, and certainly not the best, of period styles are made these days. Many of the items available in the traditional style are adaptations of originals or poor imitations. Some are reproductions of reproductions, resulting in a loss of original detail.

CHOOSING THE RIGHT STYLE

In addition to manufacturing methods, style and form are important considerations in choosing decorative brasses. Modern furniture styles are often notable for their lack of visible hardware, and woodworkers with contemporary leanings often use touch latches or sculpted wood pulls to achieve a clean look. But with traditional furniture, at least in my experience, hardware serves an aesthetic as well as a functional role, as part of an overall design.

For example, some Chippendale brasses were large and flamboyant, in keeping with the boldness of the rococo style of the time. Drawer pulls, in particular, were meant to be seen, and reflected the ornamentation of the furniture itself. On the other hand, if a particularly clean appearance was desired, such as on the doors and sometimes the drawers of a Hepplewhite sideboard, the only visible hardware might have been an inset escutcheon outlining a keyhole. Such an arrangement was often used so the hardware would not interfere with the panorama of highly figured veneers and inlaid decoration found on such pieces.

Within accepted styles of a given period, though, there is latitude in selecting hardware, depending on what effect you are trying to achieve. Even when building a special piece of period furniture, I don't want to be a slave to the perceived style of the time. I

CASTING REPRODUCES IRREGULARITIES FOUND IN ORIGINAL HARDWARE. This sand-cast Chippendale drawer pull (at right) made by Ball and Ball is thicker than the stamped version (at left). The beveled edges were filed by hand.

like to make each piece of furniture my own, as long as I can stay within the boundaries of a given period. So a Chippendale piece that was originally made with heavy rococo brasses might instead get the less elaborate button-and-bail pulls, a style that was used on late Chippendale casework. This more restrained look can be particularly effective if I pick exciting wood for the drawer fronts. Because drawer pulls varied in appearance even in the same era, I don't have to be uncomfortable about choosing a version that complements the piece I'm making. I usually opt for a more restrained look, while remaining faithful to the style.

FINISHES FOR BRASS HARDWARE

How hardware should be finished is the subject of debate. It may be highly polished or given a dull, "antique" look—a popular approach. I do not believe, however, that period hardware was anything but bright in appearance when it was new. It was meant to be seen, to turn heads. If you build reproduction furniture and want to show the intent of original makers, then antiqued hardware is the wrong choice.

Brass hardware has been coated in different ways over the centuries, to help preserve its luster and to make it look like gold. Conservation examinations have revealed evidence of different types of resin coatings on original brasses that were used to produce these effects. These coatings slowed oxidation and sometimes imparted a reddish-orange tint to the brass.

Some brasses had a coating of actual gold, created by a process called fire-gilding. Fire-gilding produced a durable, bright finish. It was costly, though, and the method of application—mixing gold powder with liquid mercury, painting it onto the brass, then burning off the mercury—is by today's standards environmentally unsound and downright unhealthy.

Today, many manufacturers coat their brass hardware with a clear acrylic lacquer. Some period hardware suppliers, however, will lacquer their products only if requested. As a general rule, I do not use lacquer on brasses that will get a lot of use. The coating can chip and, if not refinished, will oxidize and discolor in those spots. On more decorative pieces, which do not get as much wear, a lacquer coating will help maintain the shine.

EMYL JENKINS

The Chippendale Style

Chippendale. The name has a romantic, even noble, aura about it. It is a reputation that seems well-suited to the man reverently referred to as "the Shakespeare of English cabinetmakers." Flowing lines, graceful decoration, solid construction, and rich finish define the work of the man whose renown is so great that his name stands for the attributes he espoused. Chippendale is the most widely recognized name in the annals of furniture design and manufacture, and continues to be a force in furniture design to this day.

How could one man have made all that furniture? How could one man have worked in so many different motifs—Gothic, Chinese, and rococo? How did Chippendale's famed work, *The Gentleman and Cabinet-Maker's Director,* gain its worldwide reputation when other design books were also in the marketplace?

Thomas Chippendale did not build all that furniture, but he did work in many styles, and, yes, others' designs were as good as his. To put Chippendale into his proper and well deserved place in history, it is time to look at Chippendale, the entrepreneur. This 18th-century Englishman not only achieved widespread fame, he also succeeded in making "Chippendale style" as popular

in 1996 as it was in 1766. The secret boiled down to this: Chippendale captured a great look and then marketed it for all it was worth.

LITTLE IS KNOWN ABOUT CHIPPENDALE THE MAN

Thomas Chippendale was born in Otely, England, in 1718, the son and grandson of furniture craftsmen, joiners, and carpenters. He moved to London where, in 1748, he married Catherine Redshaw. As was the norm in his day, Chippendale was a furniture designer involved in the diverse skills required to furnish a house—from window treatment to fireplace design to upholstery to furniture selection. Invoices for various homes he furnished testify that he was a craftsman, designer, selector of woods, and an employer of craftsmen and specialists, from carvers and gilders to joiners and carpenters. In 1754 the first edition of his now famous *Director* was published.

How could a young man from the provinces produce the greatest and most influential furniture design book in history? The answer, according to Chippendale's biographer, Christopher Gilbert, goes back to a chance meeting between Chippendale and another young Englishman, Mattias

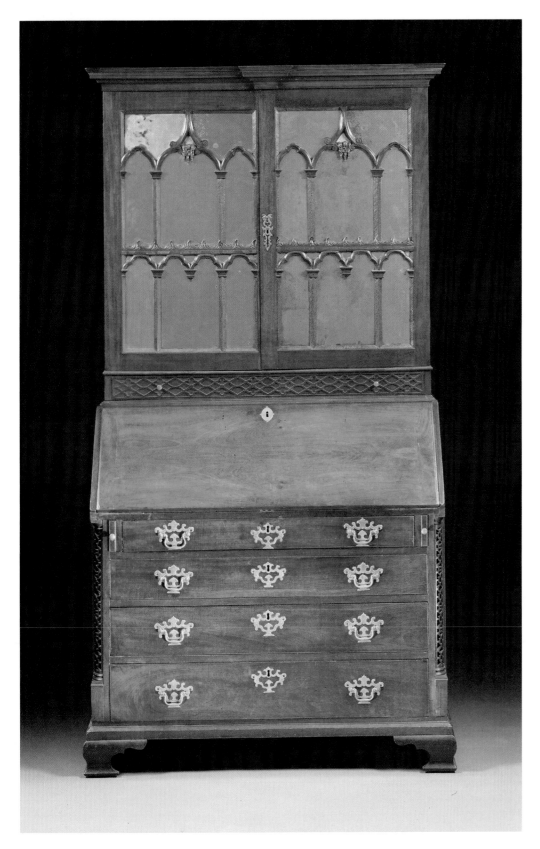

A MIXTURE OF MOTIFS. This George III mahogany bureau-cabinet combines many different Chippendale motifs: bracket feet, gothic arched mullions, pierced escutcheons, and Chinese-style fretwork and quarter-columns.

ENGLISH GENES. Free of ornamental scrolls and fretwork, this mahogany chest still has the strong linear design, shaped bracket feet, and bail brasses that today we dub "Chippendale."

Darly, an engraver, print seller, and political caricaturist. These two ambitious English chaps—one a furniture maker with a sharp eye for design, the other a talented artist aware of fashion and style of the day— came up with a great idea: a furniture design book with a new and innovative look. To give the book credibility, they found a hungry writer who penned a suitably erudite preface with exuberant references to art history and classical design. Armed with youthful boldness, Chippendale and Darly used their connections to round up an impressive list of subscribers whose names are published at the back of the book. The result: a monumental opus, *The Gentleman and Cabinet-Maker's Director* by Thomas Chippendale, with 98 of the 147 drawn plates by Darly.

THIS *DIRECTOR* HAD SOMETHING FOR EVERYONE

Actually, pictures and pamphlets of furniture designs had been around since the 16th century, but they were primarily intended for a small, elitist audience. The *Director* was different, and that's what made it so successful. Chippendale carefully included different styles for different tastes and featured almost every type of domestic furniture known at the time. Shown alongside elaborate, grandiose, and impractical (but great-looking) furniture were simpler pieces suitable for town and country houses. Instead of showing only one furniture style, as was the custom, Chippendale's book included pieces in all three of the most popular styles of the day—the rococo,

Gothic, and Chinese fashions. Finally, while some of the designs shown in the *Director* were to be made of mahogany, others were intended to be fashioned in a softwood and then gilded or japanned (painted, then varnished to simulate lacquer).

The *Director* outshone all competitive design books with its variety, comprehensiveness, and innovative designs, as well as the quality of the engravings. It became a best-seller.

The publication's fame spread so rapidly that a second edition was printed in 1755, and Chippendale continued to publish more designs that were combined into a third, larger edition in 1762. Chippendale's name was soon synonymous with the finest, most elegant furniture money could buy.

The *Director*'s unparalleled popularity inspired a rash of new design books. Some even slavishly copied the *Director* in format and design, but none equaled Chippendale's success. In March of 1763, a French edition was published. The "Chippendale look" in the form of the book, sketches, and the furniture itself was soon found worldwide. It even traveled with enterprising European settlers to Brazil, Venezuela, and Argentina.

ONE DRAWING, MANY OPTIONS. Each drawing in the *Director* gave different ornamentation options on each side of a piece, and most builders chose elements from several different drawings. The 1765 side table (below) is a rare near-replica of a single plate (left).

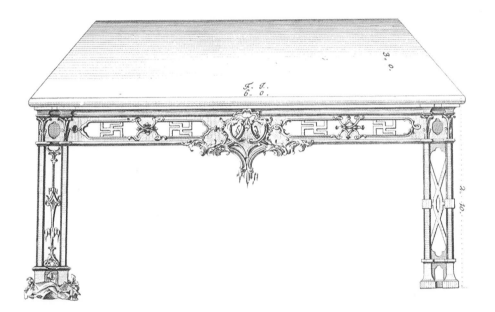

Most of the designs in *The Gentleman and Cabinet-Maker's Director* were based on the three most popular furniture styles of the time: rococo, Chinese, and Gothic. Chippendale was not the only designer to use these styles, nor did they originate with him. But the *Director* publicized them as no other publication had—forever associating Chippendale's name with these styles.

ORNAMENTATION OVERLOAD. This 1755 mahogany commode's C scrolls, apron cartouche, and carved ribbon-tied flowers and foliage characterize the rococo style.

ROCOCO

Rococo had its origins in Paris during the early 18th century. Full of scrolls, shells, jagged surfaces, and robust curves, the design was intended to imitate "rugged nature." Though the designs looked great on paper, craftsmen found the patterns difficult to execute, and the more sedate English public found the look too frivolous and sensuous when carried to the extreme. Rococo ornamentation was definitely best when used in small doses. Though Chippendale's rococo-inspired sketches are visually thrilling and probably his best known designs, little furniture of this style copied line for line was ever made.

CHINESE OR CHINOISERIE

This variation was by far the most popular of Chippendale's styles featured in the *Director*. The English had fallen in love with the exotic oriental look much earlier in the 18th century, and frequently employed pagodas, lattice-, and fretwork in their architectural designs. William Linnel, another English furniture designer, had already brought the style into favor in furniture for the home. But Chippendale carried the oriental decorative elements to their fullest and most attractive state. He took basic themes—light, feathery landscape elements, fully opened flowers, pagodas, lattice railings, and bridges—and combined them with restrained rococo scrolls to create an unforgettable look.

AMERICANS EMBRACED THE CHIPPENDALE STYLE

Meanwhile, English furniture craftsmen and designers continued to flock to America, the land of new opportunity. They took with them the latest and most sophisticated English styles, the very designs that Chippendale extolled in the *Director*. Some of the itinerant craftsmen left England's shores with no more than memories of the styles they had made or had seen being made stored away in their heads. Others brought with them rough, freehand sketches on scraps of paper.

Wealthy Americans who traveled to England returned home with stylish, new furniture purchased in London's chic cabinet shops plus copies of the new design books, including Chippendale's *Director*. Sketches derived from the books soon circulated throughout the colonies. Newspapers advertised the services of the newly arrived craftsmen and featured articles describing the current trends in furniture design. Americans' appetites were whetted.

GOTHIC

The "gothick" taste, as it was called at the time, originated in England during the 1730s and reappeared in the 19th century when archeologists unearthed medieval artifacts and writers conjured up medieval memories. Pointed arches, quatrefoil panels, clustered columns, tracery, and all types of architectural finials adorned beds, chairs, tables, even lanterns, stands, fire screens, and especially bookcases.

THE LOOK OF THE EAST. Chippendale helped popularize Asian details. This library cabinet of the period sports a pagoda-form pediment and Chinese details in the latticework and fretwork of the top molding.

MEDIEVAL MEMORIES. In this 1770 side table, the pointed arches and quatrefoils in the apron fretwork as well as the clustered-column legs show the medieval influences in the Gothic style.

Those well-to-do colonists who could not travel abroad commissioned chairs, chests, and tables like those in sketches they had seen. This furniture made in America naturally took on a slightly different look from the original English designs. After all, the local craftsmen were working within the constraints of their shops and, equally importantly, in the freer, less grand and less rigid social atmosphere of America. Ultimately American craftsmen interpreted Chippendale's basic designs and ornaments to suit 18th-century American lifestyle and philosophy.

THE STYLE WAS NEVER OUT OF FASHION FOR LONG

Furniture based on Chippendale's *Director* became the furniture of choice during the second half of the 18th century. Chippendale's original intention had been to promote himself and build up his business, but the book was more powerful than even he imagined. The *Director* broadcast Chippendale's name before the public from the Baltic to the Mississippi to the Amazon. Had he not published the book, and had the book not been so well received, Thomas Chippendale would probably be no better known than his contemporaries William Hallett, John Cobb, and Thomas Haig.

After the book was published, Chippendale's business thrived. He expanded his Maiden Lane storefront and was elected to The Society of Arts. Robert Adam, England's great architect and fellow furniture designer, commissioned Chippendale to furnish many of his finest rooms. Chippendale's work continued to receive accolades after his death.

But styles come and go. By the end of the 18th century even the Federal-like designs of Hepplewhite and Sheraton had seen their day. Regency and Empire were on the horizon, as was Biedermeier, and soon the various Victorian styles would emerge.

However, Chippendale's name and designs had staying power. English writer J.T. Smith predicted in 1828 that "as most fashions come round again, I should not wonder…if we were to see the unmeaning scroll and shellwork…revive; when Chippendale's book will again be sought after with redoubled avidity."

THE MAN BECAME A LABEL

With the dawn of the Victorian era, those rococo scrolls and shells, as well as the Gothic pinnacles and turrets, and the Chinese-influenced latticework and carving once again added just the right decorative touch. Thanks to the *Director*, Chippendale's name as well as his designs were revived.

The truth is, it was Chippendale's name, more so than accurate knowledge of his designs and furniture, that became revered a century after his death. Furniture historian John Gloag described it best: "Respect for the magic of his name was far more potent than the example of his work. To the late Victorians and Edwardians he had ceased to be a man—he had become a label." And so the all-inclusive label "Chippendale" was coined. It became such a widespread term that a turn-of-the-century writer scornfully reported that one woman, upon seeing a sketch of a dark-finished piece of furniture

SOMETHING BORROWED.
While this 18th-century Philadelphia highboy is in the Chippendale style, the only elements adapted directly from Chippendale are the finials and the scrolled pediment.

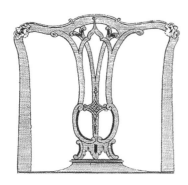

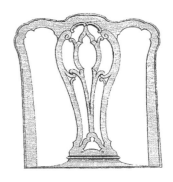

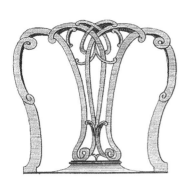

with the note that it should be "made in Chippendale," asked, "What wood is Chippendale?"

Chippendale's influence was almost as strong in the late 19th century as it had been in the 18th. The difference was that Chippendale-inspired furniture was being churned out by furniture companies and factories instead of the craftsman's workshop.

By the early 1900s, machines did most of the work, cutting and shaping the parts that were then fitted together. That cut down on time and cost. To the basic machine-made frame the early-20th-century craftsman skillfully added ornamentation and a hand-rubbed finish. Best of all, the moderately prosperous working man could afford elegant-appearing furniture, sturdy enough to last a lifetime and associated with that magical name that had come down through the ages—Chippendale.

How magical? In 1930, Emily Post wrote in her book, *The Personality of a House,* "A perfect key for one who is building a new interior would be a Chippendale

mirror.…His fretwork-rimmed tables and China cabinets, and the long-beaked bird amidst the scrolled 'C's' of his name ornamenting his gilt mirror frames, are dreams of Celestial loveliness."

The dream continues today.

(LEFT) AMERICAN CHIPPENDALE. This chair, made in the Mid-Atlantic states, is considered to be in the style of Chippendale because of the curved crest rail and the carved and pierced backsplat, but it is not a direct copy of any chair design in Chippendale's book.

LES CIZEK AND NORMA WATKINS

The Age of Mahogany

Bump along a dusty side road in south Dade County, Florida, where no tree stands higher than 20 ft. since Hurricane Andrew bored through here in 1992, and you will come upon a weedy palm grove and a stocky lumberman by the name of Mike Tisdale. In Tisdale's tarp-covered lumber stacks between the palms sits what is likely the largest stash of Cuban mahogany in the country.

Cuban mahogany means different things to different people, and it goes by many names: West Indian mahogany, Santo Domingo mahogany, and Jamaican mahogany. In the Bahamas it is known as *madeira*, in Spain as *caoba*, and on the French islands it is called *mahogany petites feuilles*. But to those with an affinity for wood, there is no mistaking it. Even salty loggers like Tisdale, who salvaged 100 tons of Cuban mahogany in the aftermath of Hurricane Andrew, will use the Latin *Swietenia mahagoni* because plain, old mahogany just won't do. "The wood is iridescent. It seems to glow a bit, like it's capturing the light," Tisdale says in his south Georgia drawl. "It glows for years."

A HURRICANE'S BOUNTY. Cuban mahogany, native only to a few Caribbean islands and south Florida, has been commercially extinct for a century. A woodworker can still acquire some from people like Mike Tisdale, who salvages ornamental trees (such as the one shown in the inset photo).

A sparsely occurring tree even before it was discovered and then decimated by European traders, *Swietenia mahagoni*—best known today as Cuban mahogany—has been used for everything from Spanish ship timbers to fuel for Havana's sugar boilers. But in the hands of European and colonial cabinetmakers during the 18th century this magnificent tree achieved legendary status. When people refer to that century as the Age of Mahogany—the golden age of European and American furniture making—it is *Swietenia mahagoni* they are talking about.

THE JEWEL OF THE CARIBBEAN

"En todas partes del mundo seria estimada esta madera (In all parts of the world this wood would be esteemed)," wrote Don Gonzalo Fernandez de Oviedo y Valdes, one of the first natural historians to visit the New World, in the 16th century. Although it would be another 100 years before it would be used widely in furniture, European explorers in the West Indies knew they had stumbled on something special. Native only to three big islands—Cuba, Jamaica, and Hispaniola—as well as parts of the Bahamas and the southern tip of Florida, *Swietenia mahagoni* could reach 120 feet, with trunks more than four feet in diameter. The timber was dense and heavy, unlikely to twist, split, or warp, and it was resistant to rot and insects. It was described in 18th- and 19th-century accounts as having an unusual luster and being cold to the touch, like stone.

The early logging of these giants sounds like a tale by Robert Louis Stevenson. Mahogany "huntsmen" would travel into the dense jungles to find the trees, no more than one or two per acre, then plot a trail out to the coast or to an inland river where

GIANTS OF THE JUNGLE. From the 1750s to today, Honduras mahogany from Central and South America has dominated the market. This photo of mahogany planks was taken in the yard of Lewis Thompson and Co., Philadelphia, in 1908.

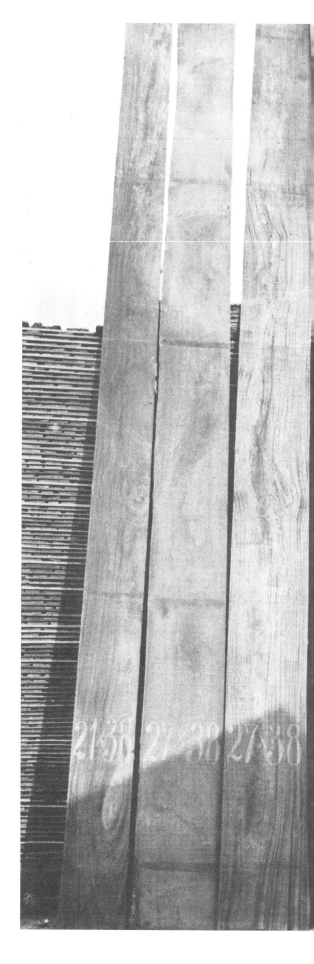

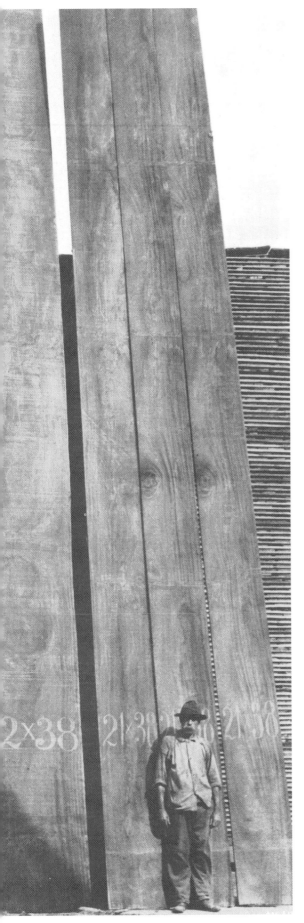

MAHOGANY WASN'T LOGGED, IT WAS HUNTED. The trees grow sparsely, about one per acre, and loggers paid "huntsmen" to find them. Logs were floated to ships or carried out by oxen.

the logs could be floated to waiting ships. Standing on scaffolding made of poles and vines, it was usually slaves who cut the trees about 15 ft. above the ground to avoid the wide buttress of the trunks. The tropical heat forced them to drag the mahoganies out at night, first by hand and later using oxen, lighting their way with torches. The logs were squared before being loaded into the holds of ships; huge amounts of timber were lost or ruined in the process.

Logging was difficult work and it was done remorselessly. Because mahogany could repel rot and worms and cannonballs with equal facility, it was a shipwright's dream. More than 100 warships of the Spanish Armada were built from mahogany. When the British man-of-war *Gibraltar* was broken up in 1836 after a century of service, its intact mahogany timbers were recycled into "Gibraltar tables"; possessing one of

"IT ASTONISHED ALL WHO SAW IT." This was the description of the mahogany brought aboard Sir Walter Raleigh's ship in 1595 on the island of Trinidad. Mahogany was also prized by carvers. This 1770s chest-on-chest by the famous Philadelphia cabinetmaker Thomas Affleck is believed to have been made of mahogany from the island of Hispaniola, now the Dominican Republic and Haiti.

THERE'S MORE THAN ONE MAHOGANY

More than 20 species are sold as mahogany in the commercial lumber market, but only two, belonging to the genus *Swietenia,* are considered true mahoganies. (A third, *Swietenia humilis*, is not sold commercially.) Most of the mahogany lumber imported into the United States today is *Swietenia, macrophylla*, called Honduras mahogany, although it probably came from Brazil. Also known as "bigleaf mahogany," it is lighter in color and weight than Cuban mahogany *(Swietenia mahagoni)*. Native only to southern Florida, Cuba, Jamaica, Hispaniola, and the Bahamas, Cuban mahogany is usually harder, heavier, and darker. Heavy logging and its limited range have made it unavailable commercially for nearly a century.

African mahogany is from the same family, Meliaceae, but it is not a member of the genus *Swietenia,* although there is a movement to reclassify it because of its similarities to Honduras mahogany. Often referred to after its genus, *Khaya,* the greatest stands occur in the Ivory Coast, Ghana, and Nigeria. The species now represents about 10 percent of the U.S. market for mahogany.

Although African mahogany sometimes is not considered a true mahogany, the word

Mahogany seedpods

"mahogany" ironically has its roots in Africa. African slaves brought to Jamaica by the British in the 17th century called the great trees *m'oganwo*. The word was later pronounced "m'ogani" (it first appeared in print in 1671) and eventually became the English mahogany.

Philippine mahogany, a less dense and much lighter—almost pink—wood from tropical Asia, is not, in fact, a mahogany at all. It is a member of the genus *Shorea*, often called "luan" or "lauan," and it can be found in almost every home center and lumberyard around the Unied States in the form of plywood. The wood is coarse and nearly impossible to confuse with real mahogany.

these was a mark of prestige for every distinguished ship in the Royal Navy.

Not all its uses were as long-lasting. In Cuba, it was used as railroad ties, fence posts, and as fuel in sugar refineries. In the 1940s, American military contractors removed nearly all the mahogany trees from Key Largo to build the hulls of PT boats, most of which were destroyed or abandoned by the U.S. Navy at the end of World War II.

It should not be surprising that *Swietenia mahagoni* did not survive our greed. "Mahogany was exploited quite heavily from the beginning, and the islands took the brunt of colonial development," says Ariel Lugo, director of the International Institute for Tropical Forestry, in Puerto Rico, a branch of the U.S. Forest Service. As early as 1629, the Spanish moved their naval shipyard from Cuba to Mexico because they had depleted the accessible stock of mahogany on the island (loggers would come back years later with improved equipment and extract harder-to-reach trees). By 1750, nearly all the mature mahogany trees in Jamaica had been cut down. By the early 20th century, supplies disappeared from the commercial trade altogether. In 1940, Cuba and other West Indian countries recognized "true mahogany" as a national treasure and embargoed its export. Luckily, much of the early wood made it into the shops of European and American cabinetmakers, whose skill helped to preserve it.

FOR CABINETMAKERS, A HEAVEN-SENT WOOD

Thank the Duchess of Buckingham and a little candle box for helping to make mahogany popular in England early in the 1700s. As the story goes (according to *The Book of English Trades,* published in the early 1800s), a British trader brought some planks of mahogany from the West Indies and left them with his brother, "an eminent physician" named Gibbons. Doctor Gibbons had his cabinetmaker build a candle box out of it and, liking the color and finish, had him build a pair of bureaus. His friends, among them the well-placed Duchess of Buckingham, found this mahogany furniture so lovely that demand for the wood was soon felt in the London timber market.

Whether this is apocryphal or true, the importation of mahogany in Europe and the colonies soared in the early part of the 18th century: the Age of Mahogany was in full flower. What made it so special? Compared to oak, elm, or walnut, mahogany timber was more stable, came in larger sizes, and was so beautiful that it was ideal for 18th-century styles. It was "the chief of furniture woods, whether considered in regard to beauty, utility, or durability," according to *The Cabinet-Maker's Assistant,* published in 1853. Its density made it a dream to carve; its tight-grained pore structure produced an unmatched luster; and its size, strength, and stability made it perfect for casework and delicate chair backs. "I can really see why they loved the wood," says David Beckford, a furniture-restoration specialist in Charleston, South Carolina. "It cuts like hard chocolate."

Perhaps most noticeable to a contemporary eye is its color: a rich red that darkened with age and was sometimes splashed with stunning figure. "It goes from salmon pink to bright orange to classic brown," says Mike Tisdale, the logger. "It's the only wood I know that gets prettier as the years go by."

A CLOSE COUSIN NOW FURNISHES THE WORLD

The age of mahogany may have been ignited by *Swietenia mahagoni,* but that is not the whole story. At the same time, traders were foraging through Central American jungles for a similar "bigleaf" mahogany, *Swietenia macrophylla,* which is lighter both in color and weight. Not as prized as its West Indian cousin, this "Honduras mahogany" was far more plentiful. Although less accessible than the Cuban mahogany, it grew wider and taller, yielding planks more than 4 ft. wide and 40 ft. long. By the 1800s, with the depletion of mahogany from the Caribbean islands, Honduras mahogany dominated the trade.

Today, most people would find it hard to tell the difference between the two (the botanical distinction was not made until 1886). Even a dendrologist looking through a microscope might have trouble. Like chameleons, mahogany trees change

SOME TREES SURVIVE IN FURNITURE. The Charleston cabinetmaker who carved this sidechair around 1750 probably used *Swietenia mahagoni* from Jamaica.

LATIN IS STILL SPOKEN IN KEY WEST. Ask a woodworker and turner like Bill Ford from Key West what real mahogany is, and he will say *Swietenia mahagoni.* Ford has spent years collecting the wood, which he uses in some of his turned bowls.

radically in response to their environment. Those growing on the dry, shallow-soiled "hammocks" of north Key Largo, for example, are heavy and dark. Landscape trees in Miami, planted with rich topsoil, grow faster but produce lighter timber that looks more like Honduras mahogany. The reverse is also true: Honduras mahogany, grown under the right conditions, can resemble *Swietenia mahagoni.* Even the African mahogany Khaya (purists will bristle at this) resembles *Swietenia* closely and may be reclassified as a result of its similarities.

Confusion existed in the 18th century as well. Timber dealers identified logs by the island or region they came from. Traders mainly were interested in the quality of specific trees, because that would determine how much money they could get for the lumber. "Sources in the 18th and 19th centuries contradict themselves all the time," says Dan Finamore, a maritime curator at the Peabody Essex Museum in Salem, Massachusetts, who has studied the mahogany trade in British Honduras, now Belize. Historians seem to agree that the majority of furniture from 1750 on was probably made of Honduras mahogany. But when Cuban mahogany did arrive from the islands, it almost always fetched a higher price.

THE PARTY IS OVER

Today, Cuban mahogany exists only along roadsides, in a few scattered plantations and in museums. Those towering trees the huntsmen climbed to locate others piercing the jungle canopy exist only in our dreams. Even trees cultivated on plantations or salvaged from the streets of Key West are not the same. Although easily germinated from large and prolific seedpods, mahogany matures best in a diversified forest. As it grows, its many predators include the shoot-borer, an insect that causes a shrubby tree, one that will never form a tall, straight trunk. Mahoganies planted in the Miami area (and there are many of them) often exhibit this low, crowded branching. "I don't think anything like (old-growth mahogany) has ever been grown since," says David Beckford of Charleston, who has worked with both the old and the new timber.

Is it still possible to find *Swietenia mahagoni* today at a lumberyard? Doubtful. "It would be like asking for the roc's egg," wrote one wistful author. If you buy mahogany today (or if you find a reproduction of a Chippendale chair) chances are you will be looking at Honduras mahogany, probably from Brazil. But it may be something entirely different; there are at least 20 woods marketed as mahogany and species have been transplanted around the globe.

A micro-market in Cuban mahogany does exist in the Caribbean and in Florida, but not enough to be sold commercially. "I doubt that *Swietenia mahagoni* will be planted for commercial use," says Ariel Lugo of the U.S. Forest Service. Dry, rocky spots produce the best timber, but it takes a long time to mature under those conditions. Grown quickly in a plantation, the diameter of a Cuban mahogany might reach one meter in 60 years—a harvestable size—but the timber would be lighter and less dense. In dry conditions, it may not reach half

that size. It is difficult to date trees in the tropics (they don't exhibit the same annual growth rings) but it is likely that many of the big island mahoganies grew undisturbed for 500 years before they were felled.

If you are lucky, you might come across a plank or two after a hurricane or in the wake of a new mall development, when salvagers like Mike Tisdale spring into action. After Hurricane Andrew, Tisdale put together a crew of workers, hustled up chainsaws and forklifts, and chased after the many "blowdowns" along streets and in the backyards of Homestead and surrounding towns, often arriving minutes before (or after) a growling wood-chipper.

"The more I picked up," he says, "the more I had to pick up." He called the salvage effort "Operation Zombie Hardwoods" after he heard a Haitian man, who was watching his crew, say: "It is a zombie. You find him dead and bring him back to life."

GIFT TO A FUTURE GENERATION. If you can't get salvaged Cuban mahogany from people like Mike Tisdale (above) you might have to wait 60 years for these seedlings (below) to reach a harvestable size. Researchers, however, do not know if Cuban mahogany can be cultivated successfully in plantations.

SOURCES FOR CUBAN MAHOGANY

Two sources for salvaged Cuban mahogany were listed in the Good Wood Alliance directory. The wood comes mainly from ornamental trees in south Florida and the Keys.

Zombie Hardwoods
S.W. 207th Ave.
Homestead, FL 33031
(305) 248-0593
$20 per board foot

Mark Butler
P.O. Box 195
Tavernier, FL 33070
(305) 664-2924
$12 to $16 per board foot

Projects & Techniques

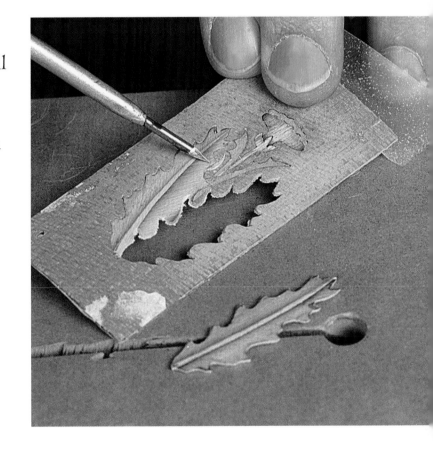

Now that you've learned about the hallmarks of the style, we'll take a look at some creative projects. Whether you want to build a drop-leaf table, a Chippendale stool, or a highboy, you'll find what you're looking for in this section. You'll also learn some techniques common to 18th-century furniture that you can apply to any of the projects here, or whatever you design on your own.

SAM FLETCHER

Making Ogee Bracket Feet

I made a stack of Chippendale-style mirrors for our annual church sale, and was disappointed when they didn't sell as well as I'd hoped. When the next sale rolled around, I looked for a more successful project. I had read that small jewelry boxes are very popular at crafts sales, so I decided to make them my next project for our fund-raiser.

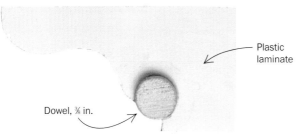

Plastic laminate

Dowel, ⅜ in.

SIMPLIFY BRACKET FEET WITH A TEMPLATE. A scrap of plastic laminate makes a good template for laying out the decorative scroll on these feet. The dowel quickly and accurately locates the template in the blank.

Boxes are simple, and they are easily made, even in quantity. But they can be awfully plain. I wanted to dress them up a bit. I liked the effect that feet add to the overall look of a jewelry box. Small ogee bracket feet elevate a box, both figuratively and literally.

High-volume shops use custom tooling to make ogee bracket feet, but my method uses a standard cove (or flute) cutter and basic hand and machine tools. Although I developed this method to make miniature feet, the general procedure can be used for making larger feet as well.

MAKE A TEMPLATE AND GLUE JIG FIRST

Decorative scrolls on the wings of these miniature feet give them a distinctive Chippendale look. To speed the layout of this scroll, I made a template from plastic laminate and a small piece of ⅜-in. dowel (see the photos at left). The dowel registers the template in each foot blank, saving me the trouble of locating the profile each time. The template also makes the feet consistent.

It can be tricky to glue small mitered pieces, so the simple jigs I make from 2-in.-sq., 1-in.-thick oak pieces are a great help (see the bottom photo on p. 51). I bore

BRACKET FEET GIVE A BOX NEW STATURE. These feet can be made easily and in any size.

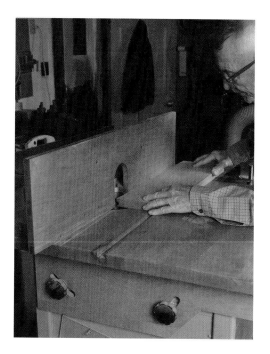

A COVE CUT IS THE FIRST STEP IN DEVELOPING THE PROFILE. The author makes a ⅜-in. cove on both edges of a piece of stock.

a ¼-in. hole in the center of each square and cut a 90° angle out of one side. The hole permits the pieces to fit together properly and takes care of glue squeeze-out. I use a 3-in. spring clamp and a short length of ¼-in. dowel to hold the pieces together.

MAKING THE OGEE PROFILE

I use a board 6 in. to 8 in. wide, surfaced to 1 in. thick, for a 1-in.-high foot. The stock thickness corresponds to the height of the foot. To make feet for a box like the ones shown in the photo on p. 47, I use a board about 2 ft. long.

Using a wider board is faster because I can work on two edges at once, ripping

ROUND OVER THE TOP EDGE. A block plane fairs a cove into the rounded edge at the top of the foot.

them as I go. Having the extra width also makes machining the wood less dangerous.

I start by making the S-shaped ogee profile in the edge of the stock. The ogee can be very dramatic or subtle depending on how deeply I cut the groove and the size of the radius on the top edge.

I cut a groove for the concave part of the ogee curve on my shaper. For the 1-in.-high feet that I'm making here, I use a ⅜-in. cove cutter set about ⅛ in. above the table to define the base of the foot. The fence is set so the cove is ¼ in. deep. I cut the groove on both long edges of the stock (see the top photo on the facing page).

I complete the ogee by rounding over the convex portion of the profile with a small block plane (see the bottom photo on the facing page). Scrapers made from an old hacksaw blade allow me to make any final corrections in the shape before the pieces are sanded.

RIPPING THE STOCK TO WIDTH AND MITERING

Now I rip a piece of molding from each edge of the stock (see the photo at right). I set the rip fence to ⅝ in., rip one side, then flip the board around and rip the other side.

The next step is to cut and miter the pieces to length. I bought my Sears™ tablesaw new in 1940 and have made a number of useful attachments for it. One of them is an adjustable cutoff stop that eliminates the need for marking each piece.

To really make cutting and mitering easier, I made additional miter gauges out of ⅜-in. by ¾-in. steel flat bar and aluminum angle. I keep one of these miter gauges set at 90 degrees and another one set at 45 degrees.

With these two miter gauges, I don't need to stop and reset the angle. I miter-cut one end, flip the stock end for end, then miter-cut the other end. Then, using the 90-degree miter gauge and the adjustable stop, I cut the piece to length, flip the stock end for end again, and cut the other piece to length. I repeat this process until I have cut enough pieces.

RIP THE MOLDING TO WIDTH. The author cuts one edge, flips the stock around and rips the opposite edge.

WITH A SHOPMADE CUTOFF STOP, you don't have to mark each piece. Two miter gauges, set at 45° and 90°, also speed the work.

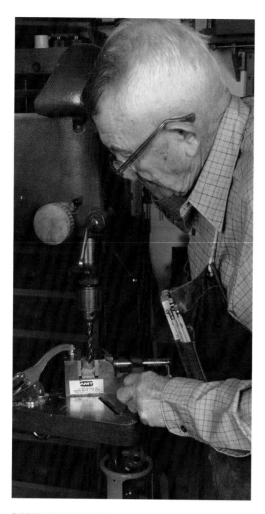

BORE THE HOLE FOR THE SCROLL PROFILE.
The hole is part of the profile and provides registration for the scroll template. A vise holds the workpiece precisely.

MARK OUT THE SCROLL. The dowel locates the template on the pieces. The profile is laid out on the back of each foot piece.

LAY OUT AND CUT THE SCROLL

The scroll at the bottom edge of the foot starts with a ⅜-in. hole bored in each piece. This hole forms part of the scroll profile, but more important, it is the reference for the scroll template. Therefore, the hole must be bored accurately. To do this, I use a machinist's vise on my drill-press table and a brad-point bit.

I separate the work into right-hand and left-hand pieces, then register one end of a piece flush with the edge of the vise jaw. To align the vise and workpiece under the bit, I place the template on the stock with the narrow end of the template flush with the square end of the workpiece.

The drill bit is lowered until it is just above the template. I position the vise so that the registration plug on the template is aligned with the bit, and clamp the vise on the drill-press table. I remove the template, bore all the like-handed parts (see the left photo, above), reposition the vise, then bore the rest.

Using the scroll template, I mark out all the pieces, as shown in the right photo on the facing page. Because the face of each foot piece already has been profiled, the scroll is laid out on the back side. I use a jigsaw to cut out the scroll shape.

GLUE JIG SPEEDS ASSEMBLY

I group all the pieces into left-right assemblies, spread glue on the mitered surfaces, and rub the pieces together. I clamp together the assemblies using the glue jig, dowel, and spring clamp. Once the glue has dried, I lightly sand the outside surface of each foot. I use a chainsaw file for smoothing the scroll. The feet are ready to be glued to the box.

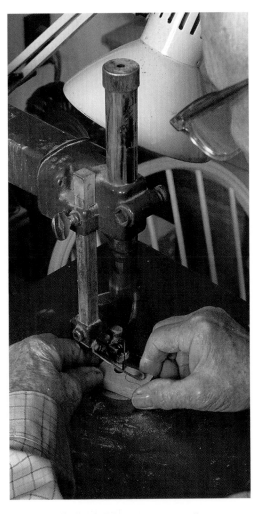

CUT THE SCROLL. The author uses a jigsaw to cut the scroll profile.

CLAMP THE PARTS. Gluing jigs hold the pieces at 90° and give glue squeeze-out a place to go. The dowel bridging the two pieces is temporary.

ROBERT TREANOR

Drop-Leaf Breakfast Table

MODESTY AND MAJESTY—
This small Queen Anne breakfast table contains a broad range of joinery. Pinned tenons, knuckle joints, and half-blind dovetails connect the aprons and legs, and rule joints run between the leaves and fixed top.

As an apartment dweller, I am constantly fighting a losing battle for space. In one small, narrow hallway in my apartment, the phone and its paraphernalia has to share space with one of the precious closets. Little room is left for a table on which to write messages or to place small items. It seemed to me that a drop-leaf table, narrow when closed, would fit the space and provide terms for a truce in my little battle. And as a peace dividend, I could always open up the table and use it elsewhere for special occasions.

The small table I made, as shown in the photo on the facing page, is a good example of a late Queen Anne breakfast table. The 18th-century form combines grace and versatility, and making it demands the same attributes in the craftsman. The half-blind dovetailed aprons, rule-jointed leaves, and the knuckle joints on the swing legs all require precise work. And shaping the compound curves of the cabriole legs needs a steady hand and eye. The skills are not difficult to master, and the effort will be rewarded with a useful and elegant table. The original on which my table is based was made of walnut, but I built mine of cherry; maple or mahogany would also be appropriate. I used pine for the small amount of secondary wood.

TAKING STOCK

Begin the table by milling the required material. Leave the leg billets slightly oversized, and set them aside for a few days so any movement can later be planed out. The pieces that will form the side aprons should be left a few inches over finished length at this point. The extra length will allow you to recut the knuckle joint for the hinge of the swing leg if necessary. Cut the fixed top and the leaves from the same board so color and figure will be consistent.

KNUCKLE JOINT IS LINCHPIN

The knuckle joints are at the heart of the table, and I start with them. The joint and the aprons it connects must be accurately

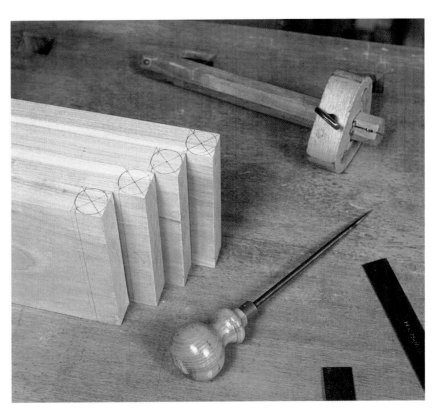

LAY OUT THE KNUCKLE JOINTS ACCURATELY, and you're halfway to a good hinge. The diagonals determine the hinge center point.

aligned to ensure the fly leg stands vertically both in its home position, where it must meet the end apron squarely, and in its open position, where it must support the leaf at just the height of the fixed top.

A knuckle joint is basically a finger joint with its fingers rounded over and the bottoms of its sockets coved. To provide a positive stop for the swing leg at 90 degrees, the joint has mating 45 degrees chamfers on both aprons, as shown in the drawing detail on p. 57. The knuckles can be cut on the tablesaw with a finger-joint jig, then finished with hand tools. With only two joints to cut, though, I opted to make the entire joint with hand tools.

Cutting and fitting the joint is not difficult, but accurate layout is essential to success. Begin the layout by marking in from the end of each piece by the thickness of the material. Then carry a line around the apron at that point. Draw diagonal lines in the square you've created on the top and bottom edges of the stock, and draw a circle, as shown in the photo above.

RUN A RABBET PLANE ALONG A GUIDE BLOCK to cut the chamfer that limits the swing of the knuckle joint hinge.

SCOOP OUT THE CENTER SOCKETS with a straight chisel. Cove the outside sockets with a gouge of appropriate radius.

The short section of the diagonals between the circle and the original layout line is the chamfer line. To make chamfering easier and more accurate, you'll need a relief cut. Draw a line parallel to the first layout line, and score along it with the corner of a sharp chisel guided by a square. Then chisel a shallow V groove on the side of the line nearest the end of the board. The groove provides a channel for your saw to ride in as you start the relief cut. Make the relief cut with a tenon saw or dovetail saw, stopping just as the kerf touches the circle laid out on the edge of the board. Now make a guide block beveled at 45 degrees, and ride a rabbet plane on the bevel to cut the chamfers, as shown in the photo at left.

Shape the barrels of the hinge with chisels and a block plane. Refer to the circles on each edge of the board as you proceed. Begin the rounding by planing a series of facets from end to end. Continue cutting narrower facets until the barrel is round. You could also use a router for some of the rounding over. A piece of scrapwood can be coved to the same radius as the barrel and used as a sanding block for final smoothing.

Lay out and cut the sockets between the knuckles next. Divide the board into five equal units across its width, and extend the division lines around the barrels. Using a backsaw, cut down the waste side of the lines to the chamfer, and then chop out the waste material with a chisel, as you would when cutting dovetails, working from both sides to avoid chipout.

The bottoms of the sockets must be coved so they mate with the radius of the knuckles. Use gouges that match the sweep of the cope for the end sockets and a straight chisel to shape between the knuckles, as shown in the photo at left.

I used a piece of $\frac{3}{16}$-in. drill rod for the hinge pin. A length of brazing rod or dowel rod would also work. To drill the hole, assemble the joint on a flat surface, and clamp it together end to end with a pipe clamp. Then clamp the whole assembly to a fence on the drill-press table, and drill the hole. To avoid bit wander, drill a little more than halfway through the joint, then flip the assembly and complete the hole from the opposite edge.

Drive the hinge pin into the joint, and check the action of the hinge. It should move smoothly without binding or much squeaking. When the joint is open to 90°, the two chamfers should form a gapless line. Set the aprons on a flat surface to ensure that they sit perfectly flat both when in line and at 90 degrees

JOINING LEGS AND APRONS

It is best to cut the leg-to-apron mortise-and-tenon joints before shaping the legs. With the legs square, the whole process is easier and more accurate. The fly legs each have one mortise and the fixed legs have two. I cut the mortises with a plunge router, holding the legs in a simple box on which I guide the router. You could also chop them by hand or with a hollow-chisel mortiser. I find it quick and efficient to cut the tenons with a dado head on the tablesaw. For these tenons, which are ¾ in. long, I stacked the dado set ¾ in. wide and made the whole cut in one pass.

The end aprons have a tenon cut on one end and a half-blind dovetail on the other. Start the dovetailing by laying out and cut-ting the tails on the pine inner apron. Then use the tails to lay out the pins on the end apron. Before putting the end aprons aside, cut the ogee detail on their bottom edge.

CABRIOLE CURVES EMERGE

Named after the French dancing term for a leap, cabriole legs do give furniture a certain vitality or spring. And they're not all that difficult to make. A small portion of the work is done on the lathe—the foot and the pad beneath it. The rest of the shaping is done with the bandsaw and hand tools.

The leg blanks have been milled square and mortised by now. Leave the horn at the top (the extra inch that reduces the risk of a split during mortising) to provide waste for chucking on the lathe. Make a full-sized template of the leg out of thin plywood or poster board, and use it to lay out the cabriole curves on the two adjacent inside surfaces of the leg. Then cut out the legs on the bandsaw. Cut the curves only; don't cut out the post block (the section above the knee) until you've turned the feet. If you were to cut away the post-block waste now, it would be difficult to center the leg blank on the lathe. When you've cut one curve, tape the cutoff back into place, and cut the second face (see the photo below).

BILLET REBUILT—With the blade guide lowered to just above the stock, bandsaw along the layout lines. Tape the cabriole cutoffs back in place, and turn the billet 90° to make the second pair of cuts. After turning the foot, clean up the bandsawn curves with a spokeshave.

SHAPING THE FOOT—Only the lower part of the foot and the pad are shaped on the lathe. To provide good purchase for the live center, leave the leg full-sized above the knee until after turning.

SHAPE AND BLEND THE CURVES OF THE CABRIOLE LEGS with rasps and files. The leg should be round at the ankle and square with rounded corners just below the knee.

Untape the cutoff, and mount the leg between centers on the lathe. Then turn the major diameter of the foot. Measure up from the bottom ¼ in., and use a parting tool to establish the pad of the foot. With the major and minor diameters defined, use a small gouge or a scraper to shape the foot's profile, as shown in the photo at left. Finally, before removing the leg from the lathe, sand the foot. Then you can take the legs to the bandsaw and cut away the waste above the knee.

The remainder of the leg shaping is done at the bench with an assortment of hand tools. You can hold the leg with a bar clamp clamped in your bench vise. The first step is to fair the bandsawn curves with a spokeshave. Be particularly careful working at the top of the foot because this is end grain and will chip easily. The front arris of the leg, though it moves in and out, should be a straight line when seen from the front. Once the spokeshave work is complete, use a cabinetmaker's rasp to cut chamfers on the corners of the leg. Leave the corners sharp in the area above the knee. Next use the rasp to round over the chamfers and blend the curves of the leg, as shown in the photo at left. The cross-section of the leg should be circular at the ankle and square with rounded corners just below the knee. When you've finished the coarse shaping with the rasp, refine the curves with a file. Further smoothing can be done with a hand scraper and sandpaper.

Next shape the knee to provide a transition between the leg and apron, as shown in the drawing on the facing page. Lay out a curved line from the top of the knee to the point where the apron joins the leg. Then cut away the waste above the line with a

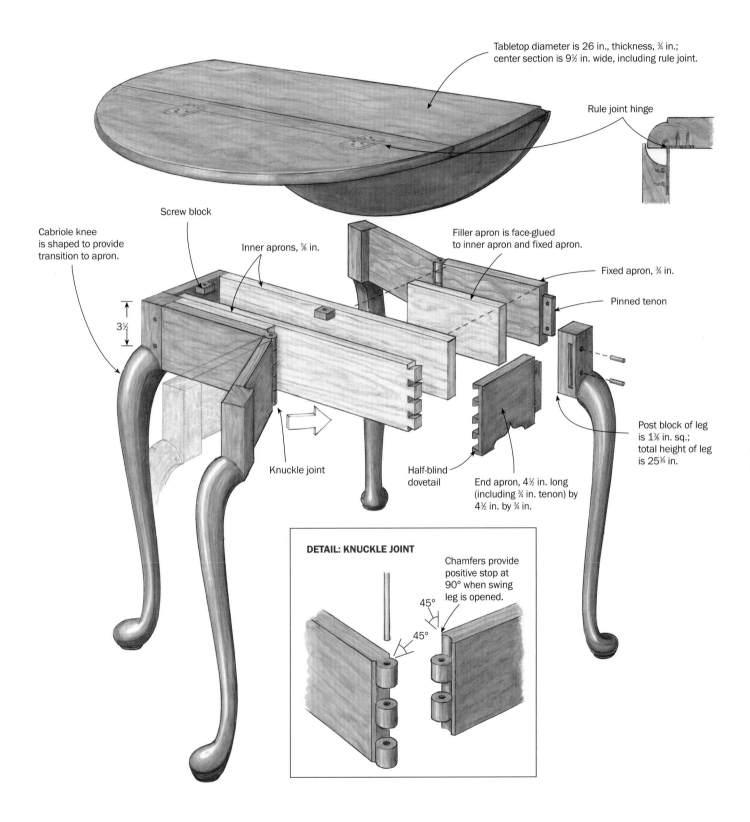

Tabletop diameter is 26 in., thickness, ¾ in.; center section is 9½ in. wide, including rule joint.

Rule joint hinge

Screw block

Cabriole knee is shaped to provide transition to apron.

Inner aprons, ⅝ in.

Filler apron is face-glued to inner apron and fixed apron.

Fixed apron, ¾ in.

Pinned tenon

3½

Knuckle joint

Half-blind dovetail

End apron, 4½ in. long (including ¾ in. tenon) by 4½ in. by ¾ in.

Post block of leg is 1⅜ in. sq.; total height of leg is 25¼ in.

DETAIL: KNUCKLE JOINT

Chamfers provide positive stop at 90° when swing leg is opened.

45°

45°

sharp bench chisel. With the same chisel, shape the knee in a smooth curve. Once the shaping of the legs and knees is complete, saw the horns from the legs. Give all the parts a final sanding, and you are ready to glue up the table base.

ASSEMBLY AND SUBASSEMBLY

With 10 separate pieces comprising its apron, this table presents an unusual challenge in the gluing up. The way I do it, there are three stages. First glue up the half-blind dovetail joints that link the end aprons to the inner aprons. Make sure the aprons meet at exactly 90 degrees before setting them aside to dry. Next glue one fixed and one swing leg to each of the hinged aprons. A bar clamp with pads on the jaws will work well. To keep the hinge from pivoting, use handscrew clamps with light pressure to clamp the hinge to the bar clamp. Set all four subassemblies aside to dry overnight.

To complete the base assembly, you'll need two filler aprons made from secondary wood. They are face-glued between the fixed section of the hinged apron and the inner apron (see the drawing on p. 57). The fit has to be perfect, so dry-assemble the subassemblies, measure the gap and mill the filler apron at that point. Glue the filler apron between the inner and outer aprons, keeping all three aligned with brads or biscuit joints.

The final glue-up is best done with the base upside down on a flat table. While the pieces are dry-clamped, check that the hinge will open through its range unimpeded. Then glue up the last two apron-to-leg joints. After the glue-up, pin all the mortise-and-tenon joints with ¼-in.-dia. pegs.

RULE JOINTS

I cut the rule joints that connect the leaves and the fixed top before roughing out the circular shape of the top. I do mill the boards carefully, though, and scrape or plane off the millmarks before cutting the rule joint. I find it easiest to cut the joint on a router table. First cut the roundover on the fixed top with a ½-in. roundover bit. Guide the top against a fence, and make trial cuts on scrapwood. Leave a ⅛-in. fillet at the top of the cut. Then chuck up a ½-in. core-box bit, and cut the leaves to fit the fixed top.

When installing the rule-joint hinges, leave some leeway for the top to expand and contract with variations in humidity. Instead of aiming for a joint that will close entirely on top, offset the hinge barrels ⅟₆₄ in. to ⅟₃₂ in. toward the leaf.

Once the hinges are in, lay out the top's diameter on its underside. It can be cut out by hand or with a bandsaw or a sabersaw. Scrape and sand the edge to remove the sawmarks, and shape the edge to a slight belly with planes, files, and sandpaper. Give the top a final sanding, and attach the base to it with screws driven through slotted holes in screw blocks attached to the inner aprons.

I finished the table with several coats of a tung oil/Danish oil mix. A coat of paste wax was applied after the oil finish was completely dry. Make sure the underside of the top and the inside surfaces of the aprons receive the same amount of finish as the visible surfaces. If you skimp on finish underneath, the table will take on and lose moisture unevenly and could be prone to warping.

PHILIP C. LOWE

Making a Sheraton Bed

Beds often are very simple, even if they look as complicated as the Sheraton bed in the photo on p. 61. The joinery isn't complicated, and there aren't many parts. In fact, once you've made the posts for this bed, the hard work is behind you. Think about the posts as different circular-shaped moldings stacked on top of one another. The posts can be made in one piece, as I do, or made in several pieces, which are glued together later. The posts also can be made without decorative reed-ing, which cuts out many hours of work on the project and still results in a pleasing design.

I always make full-scale drawings for pieces that I'm about to make. For this bed, I have to draw only one of the posts, half the shape of the headboard, and the joinery detail for the rail-post connection. I use the drawing to make a story stick (a scrap of wood where dimensions and profiles are marked), so laying out the bedposts is both easy and accurate.

TURNED POSTS ARE THE MOST DRAMATIC FEATURE OF A SHERATON BED. The posts can be turned in one piece, as the author did here, or turned in two or more pieces, which are glued together later.

■ 59

Mounting the Blank

The bedpost blanks are milled to 3½ in. sq. from 16/4 stock and rough cut to length, leaving a couple of inches at each end for mounting in the lathe. Turning the full-length blanks is no problem on my lathe, with its 10-ft.-long bed. But if you don't have this luxury, you will have to turn the post in sections, and join them together by boring a hole in one part and turning a mating tenon on the adjoining member. The joints should be cemented with yellow glue or epoxied for extra strength. I've marked a few joining points, as shown in the drawing below. As a rule, the best place to join these parts is at a fillet above or below a cove, torus, or ogee shape.

I mount the blank at the headstock end with a faceplate and plywood disc drive center, which provides a more positive drive than a spur center. This arrangement also lets me add an indexing wheel (see the sidebar on p. 65) and makes it easy to remount the blank.

The drive center is a circular piece of ¾-in.-thick plywood screwed to the faceplate. The plywood has a square hole the size of the turning blank cut out of its cen-

ter. To mount the blank, one end is slipped into the square hole, and the ball-bearing center in the tailstock is slid into position at the opposite end and locked in place.

Turning the Posts

The first step is to locate the post block, which is the nonturned section of the post into which the side and end rails are mortised. I scribe shoulder lines around the post, and with a backsaw, cut kerfs on all four corners at the shoulder points. The kerfs prevent the square edges of the post block from chipping when I turn the adjacent sections. After turning the post to the largest possible cylinder above and below the post block, I lay out and turn the pommels (the curved shoulders at the top and bottom of the post block).

To lay out the elements of the posts, I make up two story sticks or rods, one for the section above and one for the section below the post block. On the story sticks, I draw half the profile of the post and mark the diameter of each design element. I cut notches into the edge of the story stick with a skew chisel to make sure the pencil

Sheraton Bed

Posts can be turned from a single length of wood or made in pieces and glued together later.

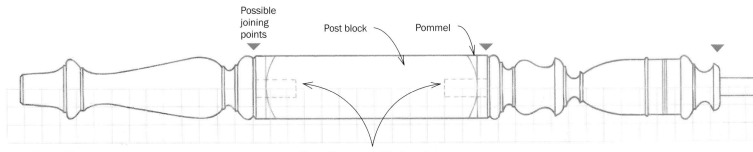

Possible joining points

Post block

Pommel

1 sq. = 1 in.

Turned tenon and drilled mortise

A SHERATON-STYLE BED IS
EASY TO MAKE, DESPITE ITS
COMPLICATED APPEARANCE.
Reeding is time-consuming but
optional, and the joinery is
straightforward. On this bed,
the author skipped the reeding
on the less prominent headboard posts.

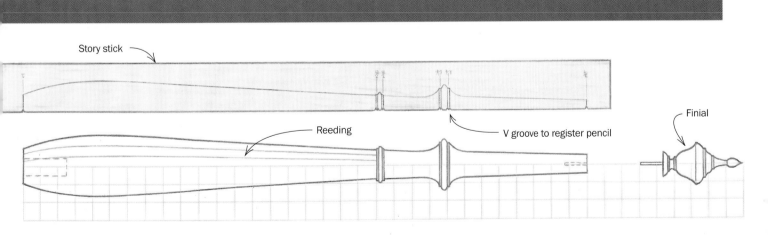

Story stick

Reeding

V groove to register pencil

Finial

references are made from the same spot when each of the four posts is laid out.

I usually hold the story stick against the revolving blank to scribe the post. Another method is to mark the post with the story stick, as shown in the photo below. Then turn on the lathe, and hold the pencil point at the mark to extend the reference line completely around the post.

I shape the bottom of the post first, turning the cylindrical blank down to the diameters indicated on the story stick with a parting tool. I check each blank's diameter with calipers. Then I shape the curves and hollows with skews and gouges, leaving the cove or scotia cuts for last. Because the coves create the smallest diameters, leaving these cuts until the end helps to reduce vibration while turning the rest of the post.

The upper section of the post is turned in the same fashion, except I add a steady rest, as shown in the photo on p. 59, to help prevent the post from vibrating and being thrown out of round when turning. After I've turned this section to as accurate a cylinder as possible, I locate the steady rest at the bulbous section of the reeded portion of the post. With the steady rest in place, the upper section is turned to shape, again leaving the coves till last.

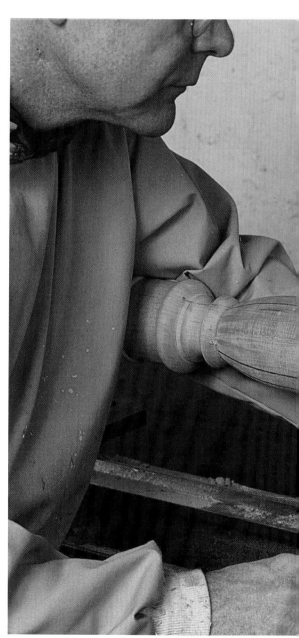

USE A STORY STICK TO LAY OUT ACCURATE AND CONSISTENT TURNING DETAILS. And the story stick is a handy reference when turning because the shape and diameter of each post section is drawn right on it.

Once I've turned the posts to shape, I sand them, starting with 120-grit and working up to 220-grit. Between each sanding, I wet the post and let it dry to raise the grain. I sand everything but the section of post to be carved with reeds because the sanding grit would get in the pores of the wood and dull my carving tool.

REEDING THE POSTS

Because it takes about four hours to carve the reeds into each post, clients frequently choose to save money by eliminating the reeding entirely or by having just the posts of the footboard reeded, as shown in the photo on p. 61. Usually, these posts are prominently displayed near the middle of the room, and the headboard posts are generally pushed against a wall.

A SCRIBE LAYS OUT EVENLY SPACED REEDS. With a pencil set to the center of the lathe and its base riding on the lathe bed, a scribe accurately draws layout lines for reeds on the top of the bedposts.

I've found the easiest way to lay out and carve the reeds is right on the lathe. To do this, though, you need an indexing wheel to hold the post in position for scribing the layout lines and carving the reeds. This is a standard feature on some lathes, but not mine, so I added one, as discussed in the sidebar on the facing page.

I also made a scribe for drawing the layout lines. The scribe rides on the lathe's bed and has a pencil set to the center height of the lathe. I mark one reed, as shown in the photo on pp. 62–63, rotate the post and mark another until the post is completely laid out. I use a V carving tool to carve lines into the post and a series of straight and back-bent gouges to carve the reeds to their half-round shapes. When carving is complete, I sand the reeds.

PUTTING IT ALL TOGETHER

After taking the post from the lathe, I drill a hole in the top of the post for a pin that will hold the finial in place and lay out and cut the mortises. There are two on each post block to accept the tenons for the rails and two more in each headboard post.

The holes for the bed bolts are staggered, so the bolt for the end rail doesn't interfere with the bolt for the side rail. These ⅜-in.-dia. holes have a 1-in.-dia.

DRILLING HOLES FOR BED BOLTS. Holes bored through the bedposts serve as guides when drilling rails for the bed bolts. The nut is hidden in a mortise in the side of the rail.

counterbore to bury the head of the bolt. I bore the holes on the drill press, starting with the 1-in.-dia. counterbore and then the ⅜-in.-dia. bolt hole, aligning the bit with the center point of the counterbored hole.

I hand drill the bolt holes into the ends of the rails, using the holes in the posts as a guide, as shown in the photo above. Mortises for the nuts are cut into the sides of the rails, so they intersect the bolt holes.

The faceplate and plywood drive center that I use to turn my bedposts make the perfect mounting system for an indexing wheel. My indexing wheel is made by cutting a hole in the center of a 10-in.-sq. piece of ¼-in.-thick plywood. The hole fits the turning blank.

After laying out the required number of divisions (16 for the bedposts) on the plywood with a compass, I bandsawed the plywood into a 10-in.- dia. circle. And I cut out the center square on the jigsaw.

Around the perimeter of the disc at each division line, I made a bandsaw cut 1 in. in from the edge of the disc. The indexing wheel is now ready to be slipped over the end of the post and then screwed to the faceplate and disc drive (see the photo below).

The stop that engages the kerfs on the indexing wheel is simply a discarded piece of bandsaw blade with the teeth ground off. This stop is held even with the centerline of the lathe by an L-shaped plywood bracket, as shown in the drawing below.

To scribe lines or carve the reeding, I pivot the stop into a sawkerf to hold the post in position. To mark or carve the next and each consecutive line, I slide the stop back and rotate the post to the next sawkerf in the wheel. I slide the stop into place and scribe or carve the next division line.

■ Indexing Wheel

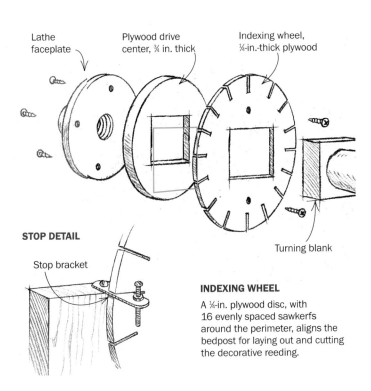

Lathe faceplate

Plywood drive center, ¾ in. thick

Indexing wheel, ¼-in.-thick plywood

Turning blank

STOP DETAIL

Stop bracket

INDEXING WHEEL

A ¼-in. plywood disc, with 16 evenly spaced sawkerfs around the perimeter, aligns the bedpost for laying out and cutting the decorative reeding.

ACCURATE INDEXING FOR REEDING.
A disc of ¼-in. plywood makes an indexing wheel for laying out reeding on the bedposts. The stop is a piece of bandsaw blade mounted even with the lathe center.

JOHN M. VAN BUREN

Veneering an Ellipse

Much of the fun and challenge of woodworking, for me, comes from copying fine examples of 18th- and early-19th-century cabinetwork. Creative purists may malign this process of imitation, but these labors have provided furnishings of incomparable design for my home, without the financial outlay that purchasing antiques would have required.

The Sheraton-style card table is a case in point. I reproduced a pair of these tables from a photograph of one in The Metropolitan Museum of Art in New York City. I wanted to use mine as side tables—not game tables—so I made them without a second hinged leaf.

The oval in the center of the serpentine apron presented a technical challenge. After some experimentation, I discovered that veneering the oval with a border of black and satinwood inlays could be done with simple equipment and a little practice.

You need to start with a master pattern: a full-scale ellipse made with ¼-in. plywood cut out on the bandsaw and then sanded smooth around the edges. This master

serves as a pattern to cut out the elliptical veneer field and as a bending form for the inlay borders.

Draw an ellipse to the required dimensions. In this case, the satinwood oval has major and minor axes of 9 in. and 2½ in. With the 1⁄16-in. inlay borders, or stringing, it is possible to bend to curves with as little as a ½-in. radius, like the ends of the one on the table shown below. The pattern is mounted on a second piece of ¼-in. plywood, about ⅜ in. larger all around, to serve as a clamping surface. Both pieces are, in turn, screwed to the edge of a block of ¾-in. wood that's wide enough to be held in a vise.

HEAT AND MOISTURE DO THE JOB

Dampen the borders by leaving them rolled in a wet towel for several hours. The dye in ebonized stringing leeches out with soaking, so it's important to keep it separated from the satinwood because it will stain the lighter veneer.

I use an ordinary laundry iron, set between "wool" and "rayon," to heat the damp veneer for bending. With the bending form set in the vise, start the borders near the middle of the ellipse, and spring clamp them to the lower piece of plywood. Using the tip of the hot iron, heat the line until it steams. Nudge it against the pattern, and secure it with another spring clamp, working around the ellipse a little at a time. Be sure to heat the line well before attempting to bend it, or the inlay will fracture. Bend the ½-in.-radius curves on the ends in small increments, and clamp the borders to the pattern as tightly as possible. Flatter parts of the ellipse will need fewer clamps. After bending the inlays around the pattern, allow the ends to overlap for trimming. Keep the tip of the iron clean by rubbing it with steel wool.

Exactly when you bend the inlay after heating it is critical, and you may need some practice to get it right. If the 1⁄16-in. stringing is poorly made, it may fracture along a grain line. If so, try another piece. When the outline of the ellipse is completed and clamped, allow it to dry overnight. In the meantime, cut out the ellipse around which the stringing will be laid up. I mark the veneer in pencil using the ¼-in. plywood template. The African satinwood veneer I used for this project cut neatly with scis-

VENEER WORK MAKES THE TABLE. This Sheraton-style table relies on intricate veneer work for the finished look.

sors. The two pieces of stringing will spring open somewhat when the clamps are removed, so they should be secured at once to the elliptical field with veneer tape or gummed craft paper. Pressing the entire inlay between flat surfaces, weighted down, will prevent curling until the ellipse has been laid up to the background.

The mahogany background was made as a frame from 2-in.-wide pieces of veneer. The veneer was taped together so that the grain pattern radiates from the center of the ellipse. Mark the cut with your actual veneer pattern, and make the cut into the background frame with a sharp razor knife.

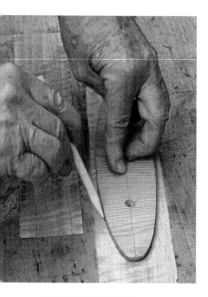

BENDING FORM IS ALSO MASTER PATTERN. The smaller piece of ¼-in. plywood can be used to mark the veneer.

BEND TWO AT ONCE. Dampened light and dark inlay pieces are bent in pairs, as they'll appear around the ellipse.

WORK IN SMALL INCREMENTS. With a tight radius, the author heats and bends only about ¼ in. at a time.

AFTER BENDING THE INLAY completely around the form and clamping it in place, allow it to dry overnight.

ONE CLEAN STRIKE WITH A RAZOR cuts the inlay for an angled seam that will virtually disappear when finished.

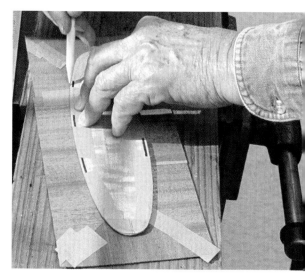

MARK EACH PIECE SEPARATELY. A completed ellipse is used to mark the cutout in the background veneer.

RANDALL O'DONNELL

Oval Chippendale Stool

It's real easy to get excited about making a stool like this. Compressed into this little gem are the chief hallmarks of the Colonial Philadelphia chairmakers: finely carved feet on graceful legs tenoned into a thin curved frame, topped off with an upholstered slip seat. Less than a handful of original oval stools exist today. To my eye, this Chippendale-style stool commands a presence far beyond the small amount of material needed to build it.

With its curves, carving, and fine proportions, 18th-century-style furniture is hard to ignore. Over the years, I've built all kinds of things from wood, but making furniture in this style continues to offer the most satisfying challenge. That challenge lies not just in the cutting and carving but in researching the history and construction details of the piece.

In my part of the country, there are not a lot of original examples of this type of furniture to examine, so to capture the essence of a particular piece, I have to do a lot of homework. First I read all of the related books and magazine articles I can find. Then I travel to check out similar pieces in museums or, if possible, in private collections. The research is far more time-consuming than actually making the piece.

This stool is an outstanding example of the Philadelphia Chippendale school of chairmaking. For chairs with curved seats, Colonial Philadelphia chair makers tenoned the legs up into a stout frame. In most

other areas, chairmakers tenoned the frame members into the leg the same way a table's aprons are tenoned into its legs; that resulted in a strong joint but a wide frame. The Philadelphia approach sacrificed just a little bit of strength for an elegantly thin frame.

Although making a curved frame and attaching curved legs may appear daunting, the joinery is dirt simple. In this article, I'll describe how to construct the frame and make and carve the legs. I'll also show you a foolproof assembly process and touch on applying the finish.

MAKE FULL-SIZED PATTERNS AND A RABBETING TEMPLATE

Start by making full-sized plywood patterns of the seat frame, leg, and knee block (for dimensions, see the drawings below and on the facing page). Additionally, you'll need to make a template to guide the router for wasting away material to form the rabbet for the slip seat.

The frame pattern provides the curve of the oval and the mortise location for the leg tenon. To avoid cutting errors, enlarge this quarter-segment pattern to full size and use it to make a complete oval pattern. Mark out one quarter of the oval, and then, using the centerlines as reference marks, flip the pattern over to mark out the remaining quadrants.

I make a plywood router template for rabbeting the frame for the slip seat. When sizing the oval opening in the template, figure in the offset between the router bit and the guide bushing you will use to cut the rabbet. Be sure to save the interior offcut from the rabbeting jig. It will be used as a router platform for cutting the bead on the top edge of the frame.

JOIN A RECTANGULAR FRAME, THEN SHAPE THE OVAL

It's astonishing that this small stool starts out with timber-frame-sized members. To build the frame, start by milling the stock to 2½ in. thick and cutting the four frame members to size. It helps to orient the frame stock so that the heart side faces down. This orientation results in an arc-shaped grain pattern that rises toward the middle of the frame, which looks much better than a slumping grain pattern.

Referring to the full-sized pattern, mark out and cut the mortises and tenons. For mortising, I use a plunge router to remove most of the waste and hand-chisel the corners and sloping transition in the mortise. A bandsaw makes fast work of the tenons. Again, I carefully pare to the layout line with a chisel.

Many original Philadelphia pieces simply left the inside of the beefy frame rectangular, but I prefer to cut away a lot of the excess bulk to reduce the mass. Prior to assembly, I bandsaw large arc-shaped hunks from the frame interior.

Now, glue up the frame. Don't worry about clamp marks on the frame edges, because they will be cut away when you saw the oval. After the glue dries, use the pat-

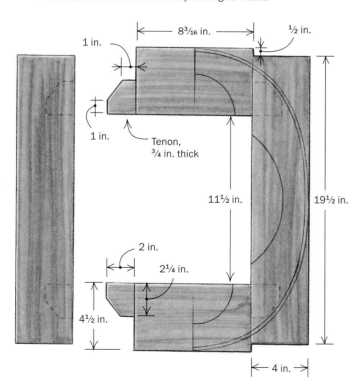

Massive Timbers and Simple Joinery

This handsome, little stool starts as a hefty rectangular frame.

8³⁄₁₆ in.

½ in.

1 in.

1 in.

Tenon, ¾ in. thick

11½ in.

19½ in.

2 in.

2¼ in.

4½ in.

4 in.

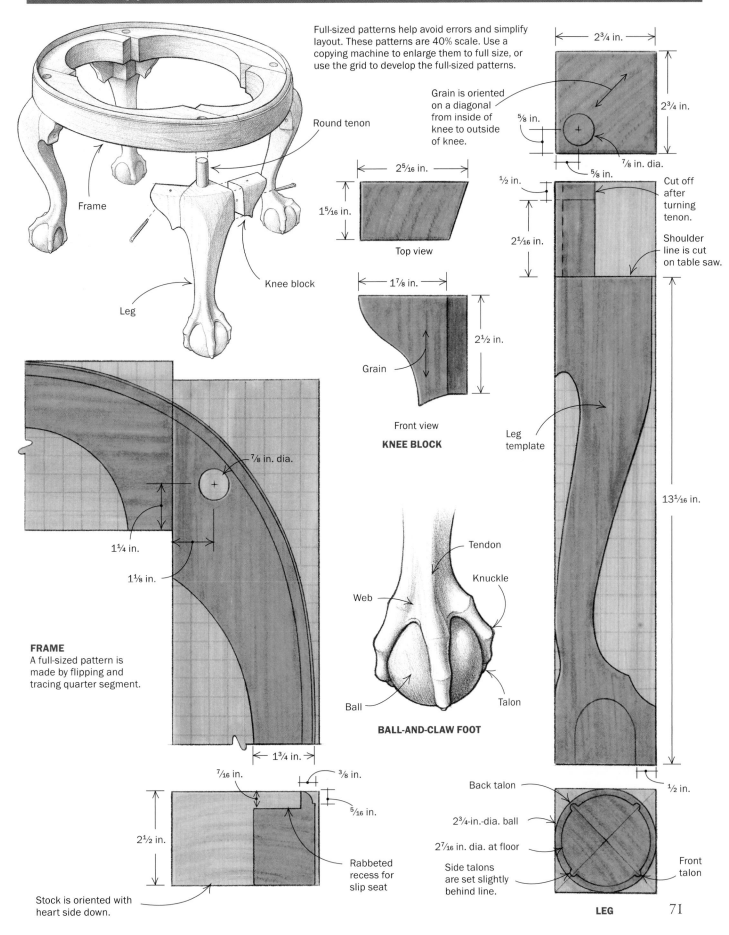

Full-sized patterns help avoid errors and simplify layout. These patterns are 40% scale. Use a copying machine to enlarge them to full size, or use the grid to develop the full-sized patterns.

Round tenon

Frame

Knee block

Leg

2³⁄₄ in.

2³⁄₄ in.

Grain is oriented on a diagonal from inside of knee to outside of knee.

⁵⁄₈ in.

⁵⁄₈ in.

⁷⁄₈ in. dia.

2⁵⁄₁₆ in.

1⁵⁄₁₆ in.

Top view

1⁷⁄₈ in.

2¹⁄₂ in.

Grain

Front view

KNEE BLOCK

½ in.

2¹⁄₁₆ in.

Cut off after turning tenon.

Shoulder line is cut on table saw.

Leg template

13¹⁄₁₆ in.

½ in.

⁷⁄₈ in. dia.

1¼ in.

1⅛ in.

FRAME
A full-sized pattern is made by flipping and tracing quarter segment.

Tendon

Knuckle

Web

Ball

Talon

BALL-AND-CLAW FOOT

1¾ in.

⁷⁄₁₆ in.

⅜ in.

⁵⁄₁₆ in.

2½ in.

Rabbeted recess for slip seat

Stock is oriented with heart side down.

Back talon

2³⁄₄-in.-dia. ball

2⁷⁄₁₆ in. dia. at floor

Side talons are set slightly behind line.

Front talon

LEG

ASSEMBLE THE FRAME. The bulk of the frame has been reduced by bandsawing arc-shaped segments prior to assembly.

A ROUTER MAKES FAST WORK OF THE SEAT RABBET. Use a full-sized oval pattern to establish the layout line.

THIS GOUGE IS GOOD. To hog away stock the router couldn't reach, the author used a gouge.

tern to mark out the ⅞-in.-dia. mortises and then drill them.

Some Philadelphia chairmakers used a separate, applied lip to house the slip seat because it was more economical. For me, it's easier to make the lip by rabbeting the frame, using a router to waste away the excess stock quickly. Using an exterior template and router guide bushing prevents cutting into the lip. Because the router base is too small to provide adequate support while cutting the area toward the middle of the frame, I use a gouge to pare away the waste. After rabbeting the frame, saw it to the oval shape on the bandsaw. I use an oscillating edge belt sander to clean up the profile to the scribe line.

An edge bead on the seat rim forms a neat transition from the frame to the slip seat. The rabbeting template offcut, placed where the slip seat goes, provides the platform for supporting the router. You could use a standard beading bit for this edge bead, but I prefer to end up with a less machined-looking result.

I first make a ¹⁄₁₆-in. rabbet around the perimeter of the frame and then round over the top edge with a cabinetmaker's file. Develop the bead by making a series of small parallel chamfers, with the grain, along the perimeter of the frame. I think the slight irregularities resulting from this process give an authentic, handworked look to the piece.

BANDSAW THE CABRIOLE LEGS, THEN TURN THE TENON

The leg material should be sound, straight-grained stock. Cut the 2¾-in. square leg billets to size. Allow an extra ½ in. of length on the tenon end for the lathe's spur center. It will be cut off after the tenon has been turned. Use a full-sized pattern to mark out two faces of each leg. Orient the pattern on the leg billet so that the resulting leg profiles are knee to knee. Mark the center point of the round tenon on both ends. To define the start of the tenon, cut the shoulder lines at the top of the knee on the table saw.

Before turning the leg, cut the cabriole shape on the bandsaw to reduce the leg mass and lathe vibration during the tenon turning. When cutting cabriole legs, I use the bridge method, to eliminate the need for reattaching the offcut stock. Briefly, when bandsawing the first cabriole profile, don't saw off the waste completely. Instead, leave a small bridge between the leg and the waste. This allows you to cut the other side of the leg profile without having to reattach the sawn-away stock. Cut through the bridge after the second profile has been cut.

Once the leg has been rough-cut, turn the tenon. Mount the leg on the lathe with the tenon nearest the headstock. The spinning blur of a leg may look a little scary, but it's quite safe because all of the work is confined to the tenon. Use a short tool rest so there's no chance of getting pinched between the leg and the tool rest (see the photos above).

CARVE THE FEET

By about 1755, the ball-and-claw foot had become firmly identified with the American Chippendale style. The motif is thought to have originated in China as a dragon's claw clutching a pearl. (See the sidebar on pp. 74–75 for details on making this feature.)

To make the feet for this stool, draw two concentric circles on the bottom of each foot. A 2¾-in.-dia. circle is the full diameter of the ball. A 2⁷⁄₁₆-in.-dia. circle is the ball

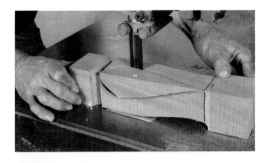

LIGHTEN THE LOAD, THEN TURN THE TENON. Rough bandsaw the leg, leaving a bridge of material to hold the first cutoff in place. When turning the tenon, use a short tool rest for best support.

diameter at the floor. Mark the equator—the horizontal centerline of the ball—⅝ in. from the bottom of each foot. Now, mark the toe outline from the drawing.

To achieve uniformity, carve the four legs together, advancing all four from one stage to the next. I use only a few carving tools to make the feet: a V parting tool, a #2 gouge, a #8 long-bent or #8 spoon gouge, a rasp, and a riffler. The tool numbers refer to the gouge's cutting-edge radius, or sweep.

Start by outlining the toes on the ball using a V parting tool. Using the #2 gouge and the V parting tool to refine the outline, cut the ball area to a cylinder by working to the layout line marked on the bottom of the foot. Then smooth this area with a rasp to produce a nice, uniform surface. With the #2 gouge, round the top area of the ball, working from the equator and deepening the toe-to-ball junction with the V parting tool. Be careful not to remove any stock from the center point of the equator—this is the basic reference for the ball diameter. Round the lower half of the ball, working down to the inner circle. Keep referring to the other three surfaces between the toes to

CARVING A BALL-AND-CLAW FOOT

1. ESTABLISH A CYLINDER

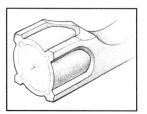

OUTLINE THE TOES WITH A V PARTING TOOL. Cut to the depth of the larger circle marked on the bottom of the foot.

SHAPE BETWEEN THE TOES. Use a #2 gouge and cut to a cylindrical form between the toes.

2. SHAPE THE BALL

ROUND THE TOP, THEN THE BOTTOM. Carve from the equator toward the ankle with a #2 gouge. Work around the ball to develop a sphere. Then carve down from the equator to shape the bottom of the ball.

3. LOCATE AND CARVE THE KNUCKLES

MARK THE KNUCKLES. The front and side toes have three knuckles; the back toe has two.

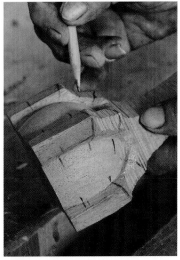

SHAPE THE TOES. Round over and slightly undercut the toes. The areas between the knuckles are scalloped and thinner than the joints.

4. CUT THE TALONS AND TENDONS

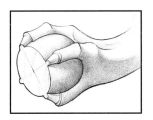

CARVE THE TALONS. Taper the talons to about ⅛ in. at the bottom of the foot. Note that the side talons taper to a point slightly behind the line.

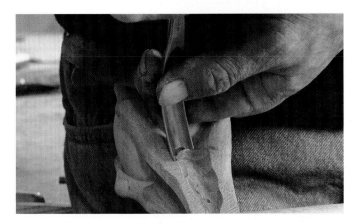

PROMINENT TENDONS PRODUCE A STRONG-LOOKING GRIP. Define the tendons and web using a #8 bent gouge. Work up from the ball to the knee.

FOUR-LEGGED UNIFORMITY. Complete each stage on all legs before moving on to the next stage. Use rifflers and sandpaper for a refined foot.

maintain the spherical shape. Once you have the ball rounded, smooth it with a riffler.

Now, mark out the toe joints: three on the front toes and two on the back. Round over the toes, slightly undercutting them at the ball surface. Scallop and thin the toes between the knuckles, making the knuckles more prominent. Once the toes have been defined and rounded, mark out the talons ½ in. from the bottom of the foot—Philadelphia-style ball-and-claw feet tend to have rather stubby talons. Note that even though the side toes are forward at the centerline for most of their length, their talons taper to a point slightly behind the centerline. The front and back talons are aligned on the centerline. Taper the talons to about ⅛ in. dia.

Now comes the part that really gives a feeling of tension in the foot: cutting the

web and defining the tendons. Use a #8 long-bent gouge and start defining the extent of the tendons. Work from the ball up toward the knee, leaving the web proud of the ball by about 1⁄16 in. Smooth the carving with rifflers and small pieces of sandpaper. Shape the leg from the ankle to the knee with a rasp and rough-sand the lower leg and foot. The upper leg will be shaped and faired to the frame in the next step.

FIT THE KNEE BLOCKS AND FAIR THE UPPER LEGS

The knee blocks make the visual transition from the legs to the frame and buttress the joint. Fitting knee blocks to a curved frame is somewhat different from the usual rectangular frame because the blocks flare away from the leg to meet the frame.

Dry-fit the legs into the frame, aligning the flat knee-block surface of the leg parallel to the frame's joint line (see the photo at left). Now, screw the knee blocks in place to hold the leg in this position for rough shaping the upper leg. Be sure to mark the legs and knee blocks so that you can return them to the same positions on the frame. Carefully remove the legs without disturbing the knee blocks.

FINISH UP

With the knee blocks still screwed in place, glue the legs to the frame. Once the glue has started to set (about 10 minutes), remove the knee blocks, one at a time, apply glue, and screw them back in place. After the glue-up, replace the screws in the knee blocks with hand-forged nails for authenticity.

After the glue dries, use a #2 gouge and a pattern-maker's rasp to blend the curves of the upper legs and knee blocks into the frame. The final smoothing is done with sandpaper, starting at 100 grit and ending with 180 grit. Sponge with water, then give the surfaces a quick hit with 400-grit paper to remove any raised wood fibers.

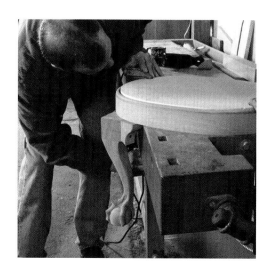

TEMPORARY FIXING. With the ball and claw complete, prepare to carve the knee by dry-fitting the leg to the frame. Use screws through the knee blocks to hold the leg in place.

KNEE WORK. With the leg dry-fitted, rough-shape the upper leg, blending the knee to the frame. Final fairing with a rasp is done after glue-up.

The knee blocks temporarily screwed to the frame ensure that the legs go back in the same position. The knee blocks are glued in place after the leg glue joint has started to set.

Susy, my patient wife, does the finishing and really gets the wood's figure to pop. She colors the wood with red mahogany aniline dye, followed by a washcoat of shellac. Two separate applications of paste filler with a black tint, spaced a day apart, follow. Finally, several coats of buttonlac shellac topped off with Behlen's violin varnish make the stool glow.

Crowning this regal little stool with a silk damask-covered slip seat completes the project. I make the frame, and an upholsterer does the webbing, padding, and fitting of the fabric. To make the frame, I simply join a rectangular assembly of poplar, bandsaw it to the oval shape ⅛ in. smaller all around than the seat recess, and cut a heavy chamfer around the top outside edge.

JEFFERSON KOLLE

Pembroke
Table

D ivorce is a nasty thing. Aside from the obvious casualty of the demise of my family, I regret the fact that Eddie will no longer be my father-in-law. Over the course of nearly 20 years, he has become one of my best friends. He always admired a Pembroke table I'd made years ago, and in fact, he commented on it almost every time he came to our house. In appreciation for all that I've learned from him—he'd been more than a surrogate father since my dad died—I wanted to make another one of the tables for him.

Pembroke tables have been around for centuries. Small and graceful, they have been made in forms simple to elaborate. The one I made is on the simple side—the only adornments being the tapered legs and the curved top. What makes the table fun to build are the moving parts: the hinged drop leaves with their attendant rule joints and the short, wood-hinged arms that support the leaves. In the drawings, I've included the dimensions for my table, which is 34¾ in. long at the center of the top. You can adjust the dimensions of the table to suit your needs. Most often, Pembroke tables are small side tables, but they were built in all sizes. I once measured an antique Pembroke table with a 48-in.-long top.

TWO-PIECE JIG IS USED TO TAPER LEGS ON THE TABLE SAW

I can't claim ever to have had an original thought, and I certainly can't claim to have invented anything as far as woodworking is concerned. The tapering jig I used for the table's legs is no exception. I borrowed the idea from Charles Grivas of West Cornwall, Conn. I'm not sure he invented it, either, but it sure works well.

The tapered legs are cut from 1⅞₆-in. square billets, 29¾ in. long (see the photos in the sidebar on p. 80). The taper starts 6 in. down from the top of each leg. The legs taper on all sides to ⅞ in. at the floor. It's a good idea to cut the mortises in the legs before you start tapering.

Set your table saw fence for about 5 in. and rip two 35-in.-long, medium-density fiberboard (MDF) or plywood scraps. After ripping, don't touch that table saw. You're going to taper the billets by setting them proud of the edge of the ripped strips and sending them through the table saw at the same fence setting, once for each tapered leg side, for a total of four cuts.

Lay out a ⅞-in. square centered on the bottom end of one of the billets and square around the billet 6 in. down from the top. Set the billet atop one of the MDF strips with the 6-in. square line and the outside edge of the ⅞-in. square flush with the edge of the MDF.

Trace the billet onto the MDF and then, using a bandsaw or jigsaw, remove the outline of the billet. After you've made the cut in the MDF, pressure-fit the billet into the

LEG TAPERING JIG IS MADE FROM TWO STRIPS OF MDF RIPPED TO THE SAME WIDTH. The edge of a ⅞-in. square marked on the bottom of a leg billet hangs over the edge of the MDF strip. The billet, held to the outside edge of the smaller square, is traced on the MDF and cut away to make a pattern for the first two cuts on the four-taper legs. Leg billets are pressure-fit into the cutouts in the MDF and ripped on the table saw.

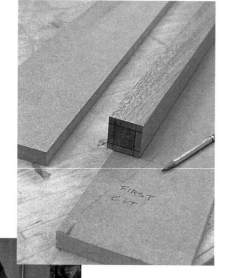

RIP THE FIRST TWO TAPERS ON ONE JIG. The part of the billet that sits proud of the MDF strip is ripped away when the MDF strip is sent through the saw at the same setting at which the strips were ripped.

COLOR CODING CAN COUNTER CONFUSION. The author marked two perpendicular sides of each billet end with a red pen for the first cuts and a green pen for the second cuts. The jigs are coded the same way. (The first cuts in the billet in the photo have already been sawn away.)

cutout, then send the MDF through the table saw.

Hold the one-taper billet to the edge of the second MDF strip, just as you did before. One edge of the ⅞-in. leg-bottom square will have been removed by the first cut. Line up the 6-in. square line again and the edge of the ⅞-in. square opposite the side that was removed with the first cut. Trace the one-taper leg onto the second strip of MDF and remove the leg outline as you did before. To distinguish the two MDF strips, and thus to avoid cutting the wrong tapers on the wrong sides—I've been known to make mistakes in my life—I made a red mark on the first-taper strip and a green mark on the other. Then I marked the end of the billets: red for the first cuts and green for the second cuts.

When you have made the cutouts on both MDF strips, you're ready to taper. Fit a billet into the first-taper strip and taper the first side. Then turn the billet and taper a side perpendicular to the first. Fit the billet into the second MDF strip and taper the two remaining perpendicular sides.

SWINGING LEAF SUPPORT PIVOTS ON A WOOD HINGE

The table's short leaves are supported by flipperlike arms that swing out of the side aprons on wood hinges and fold flush into the aprons when the leaves are down. The five-knuckle wood hinge is pinned at the centerline of the side apron with a length of ⅛-in.-dia. steel rod. Cut two lengths of 4½-in.-wide stock 6 in. longer than the finished length of the aprons. You'll need the extra length to account for the tenons and the wood you waste when making the hinge.

Mark five knuckles of the same size across the apron's width. Crosscut the apron stock through the five knuckle lines and then make a mark ⅝ in. from each end of the cut. In ¾-in. stock, a ⅝-in.-long knuckle works well. Anything longer and the hinge will bind when it's glued to the secondary-wood subapron. The swinging leaf support has two knuckles, and the stationary apron piece has three knuckles. Butt the two

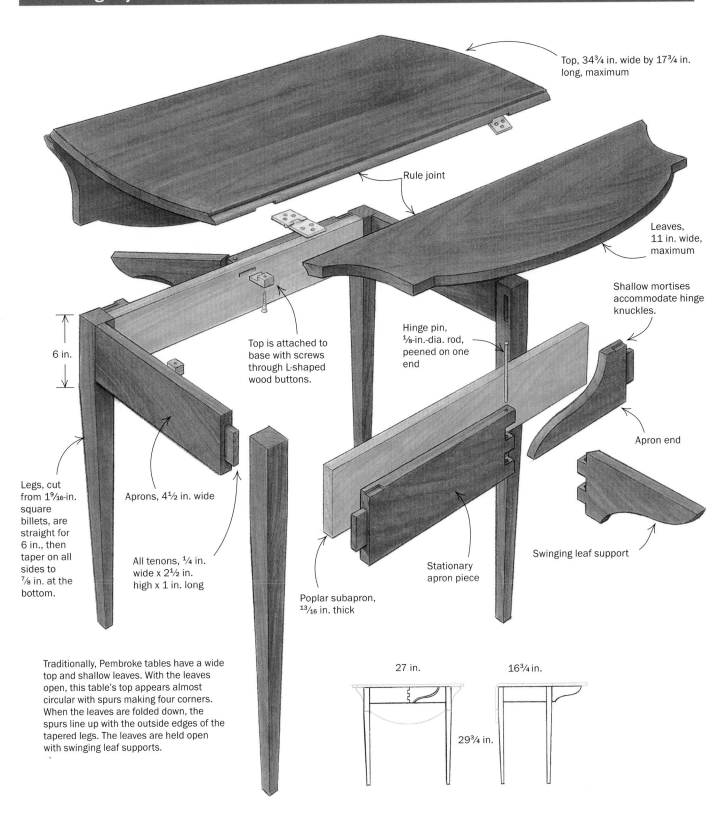

Top, 34¾ in. wide by 17¾ in. long, maximum

Rule joint

Leaves, 11 in. wide, maximum

Shallow mortises accommodate hinge knuckles.

6 in.

Top is attached to base with screws through L-shaped wood buttons.

Hinge pin, ⅛-in.-dia. rod, peened on one end

Apron end

Legs, cut from 1⁹⁄₁₆-in. square billets, are straight for 6 in., then taper on all sides to ⅞ in. at the bottom.

Aprons, 4½ in. wide

All tenons, ¼ in. wide x 2½ in. high x 1 in. long

Swinging leaf support

Poplar subapron, ¹³⁄₁₆ in. thick

Stationary apron piece

Traditionally, Pembroke tables have a wide top and shallow leaves. With the leaves open, this table's top appears almost circular with spurs making four corners. When the leaves are folded down, the spurs line up with the outside edges of the tapered legs. The leaves are held open with swinging leaf supports.

27 in.

16¾ in.

29¾ in.

marked pieces end to end and mark waste lines on each piece (see the top left photo on the facing page).

Cutting the wood hinges is exacting. To look good, the knuckles must fit tightly but should not be so tight that the hinge won't swing. Prepare to do a lot of test fitting. The back side of the hinges must be relieved at about a 45° angle so that the knuckles on one piece can swing past the knuckles on the other (see the top right photo on the facing page).

Once the knuckles fit together, clamp the two pieces to a backer board and drill a ⅛-in.-dia. hole through the center of all of the knuckles (see the bottom left photo on the facing page). Push a long piece of ⅛-in.-dia. steel rod through the hinge and test the action. Unless you're a real ace, you'll have to pare away at the knuckles to get the hinge to swing smoothly. Using a piece of long rod for the test fitting makes it easy to pull out the pin when you have to adjust the knuckles.

Each swinging leaf support has a gentle cyma curve cut into the end, and it folds flat against another, slightly more exaggerated curve cut into the apron end. Use a

gouge to relieve part of the back of the leaf support to provide a fingerhold (see the bottom right photo on the facing page).

When you are convinced that the leaf support works smoothly and you're pleased with the fairness of the curves cut on the supports and apron ends, glue the stationary part of the hinge and the apron end to a 4½-in.-wide subapron made of a secondary wood (poplar in this table). Because the primary apron is broken by the swinging leaf support, the subapron gives strength to the assembly. Gluing the apron pieces together makes it easy to cut the tenons (see the photo below).

RULE JOINTS ADD DECORATIVE TOUCH

The hinged leaves on some unadorned drop-leaf tables simply butt to the tops when folded up. Rule joints—a combination of two moldings, cove, and roundover—add a decorative and structural element to a drop-leaf table. When a table leaf is folded down and hangs vertically from the tabletop, you see a decorative, molded roundover along the edge of the top. And when the leaf is folded up, the cove in the leaf rests on and is supported by the roundover, giving strength to the joint when the table is loaded.

For the first Pembroke table I made, I borrowed rule-joint planes from Mike Dunbar, and in fact, the inspiration for this table came from his Taunton Press book, *Federal Furniture* (1986). Cutting the joint with molding planes wasn't easy; using a router table with a ½-in. cove bit and a ½-in. roundover bit was a piece of cake.

I don't think it matters whether you first cut the cove in the leaves or the roundover in the top. What's important is that you have a perfectly jointed edge between leaves and top before you cut the moldings. It's also important that the fillets—the flat, vertical section of each molding—above the roundover and the cove be the same dimension. If they aren't, the top and the leaves won't sit flush in the opened position. I used ³⁄₁₆-in. fillets on my table.

TABLE APRONS ARE DOUBLE THICK. After the swinging leaf support has been cut, fit, and drilled and the end of the apron is cut with a cyma curve, the primary apron pieces are glued to subaprons. Cutting tenons on the doubled up aprons is straightforward. In the photo, the swinging support has been removed from the apron.

THE DROP-LEAF SUPPORTS SWING ON A WOOD HINGE. Hinge knuckles—two on the support and three on the stationary piece—are ⅝ in. long. The width of each knuckle is determined by the width of the apron stock divided into five parts. A cyma curve on the end of each support adds a decorative touch.

KNUCKLE RELIEF. The back of the wood hinge knuckles are cut away at an angle so that the hinge can swing freely. If the knuckles were left square, their front sides would pinch one another as they swung.

FIT TO BE DRILLED. Once the wood hinges have been pared to fit, clamp the pieces together against a backer board and drill a ⅛-in.-dia. hole through the hinge. A ⅛-in.-dia. steel rod is used as a hinge pin.

FINGERHOLD IS CUT WITH A GOUGE. The swinging leaf support, cut on the end with a gentle cyma curve, nests against the apron end, which gets cut with a slightly more exaggerated curve. The back of the support is relieved with a gouge to provide a fingerhold for opening the support.

Trust me on this: It's a good idea to run extra lengths of scrap with the cove and roundovers run into the edges. Table-leaf hinges are a different breed of (swinging) cat, and it's a good idea to mount a pair to some scraps before you attack the real top. And later, the scraps can come in handy for tuning up the rule joints.

HINGE INSTALLATION IS EXACTING

A table-leaf hinge is unusual for several reasons: one leaf is longer than the other; the leaves are countersunk opposite the barrel; and in operation, the hinge folds away from the barrel rather than around it as it does on a regular butt hinge. The longer side of the hinge gets screwed to the table leaf.

Rule-jointed table leaves pivot not from the tabletop's widest point but rather from a point in line with the fillet on the round-over (see the drawing on the facing page). The exacting part of setting a tabletop hinge comes in setting the hinge barrel (and thus the pivot point) in line with the fillet. If you set the pivot point a little too far forward or too far back, the rule joint will

bind as it swings or the leaf will hang too low, revealing the hinge mortise. Neither case is the end of the world, and both can be remedied with a little fiddling.

Mounting a table hinge requires that the hinge barrel get mortised deep into the tabletop and the hinge body get mortised flush with both the tabletop and the leaves. Transcribe the fillet line—½ in. back from the edge of the roundover—to the underside of the top. Use a ¼-in. chisel to knock out a rough mortise for the barrel, centering the hinge pin on the line you've transcribed. Neatness doesn't count here because the hinge body will cover the barrel mortise. Once the barrel has been mortised and the hinge body rests flush with the underside of the top and leaf, you can mark around the hinge and then cut the mortise for the hinge body into the top and the leaves. Drill holes for one screw in each of the hinge leaves and attach the leaves to the top.

Set the top and leaves on the edge of your bench so that one of the leaves hangs over the side, and test the action of the hinges and the rule joint. It's likely that you'll have to fuss with the joints to get them just right. If the leaf hangs too low

Swinging Leaf Supports Apron

METAL PIN, WOOD HINGE. The top of the pin is peened to prevent it from slipping out. In operation, the swinging leaf support folds flat against the apron when the table leaves are down.

on either side or both, such that you see the hinge mortise on the underside of the tabletop, you'll have to deepen the hinge-barrel mortise on the tabletop. Don't deepen the end of the mortise on the edge of the roundover, just the barrel mortise and that area of the hinge leaf toward the center of the tabletop; you're trying to sink the hinge deeper into the tabletop and thus raise the height of the attached leaf.

If the leaf binds as it swings open—you'll hear an annoying squeaking, scraping noise—the easiest thing to do is get out the sandpaper. I used spray adhesive to attach a strip of sandpaper to one of the test scraps I made when cutting the rule joint. Use the scrap with the cove cut into it to sand the roundover and vice versa. When both leaves swing well, drill and drive in the rest of the screws.

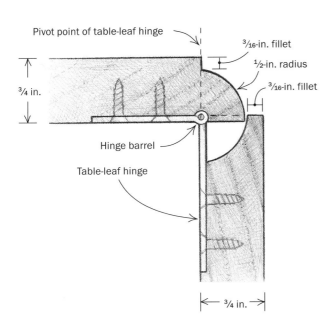

Pivot point of table-leaf hinge
3/16-in. fillet
1/2-in. radius
3/16-in. fillet
3/4 in.
Hinge barrel
Table-leaf hinge
3/4 in.

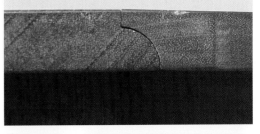

HINGE PIVOTS AT THE ROUNDOVER FILLET LINE. Transcribe a line on the underside of the tabletop equal to the setback of the vertical fillet on the rule joint.

MORTISE THE BARREL FIRST. Then scribe around the hinge leaves and mortise them flush with the tabletop.

Table   Leaf

LOOKS LIKE A BUTT HINGE, BUT IT AIN'T. A table-leaf hinge has leaves of different lengths, and the screw holes are countersunk on the sides opposite the barrel.

Trammels
Lay Out the Top

When viewed from above, the top of table looks like a circle with squared-off spurs at each corner. In fact, the edges of the table ends and the leaves are sections of a circumference each with a different center point. To my eye, one of the cool things about the table is the way the spurs on the leaves hang even with the outside edges of the legs.

With the hinges mounted and the rule joints tuned, flip the top over on your bench and find the center of the top. Mark two long axis lines through the center point, one line perpendicular to the rule joint and one parallel to it. Temporarily set the table base upside down on the top, clamp the leaves against the legs, and mark lines on the underside of the tabletop along the outside of the four legs (see the drawing on the facing page). It's a good idea to make witness lines so that you can align the table base and the top the same way in the future.

On each table-leg line, mark a point 7 in. from the rule joint. This point will become the end of the spur. Traditionally, Pembroke tables have short leaves, and although the 7-in. point is arbitrary, it's a good size for the leaves.

From that 7-in. point, mark a 1½-in.-long line perpendicular to the table-leg line, and then mark a point 1½ in. back toward the rule joint on the table-leg line. These 1½-in. squared corners will become the four spurs. Now you'll draw sections of circles between the spurs.

I made a trammel out of a pencil and a strip of wood with a drywall screw through one end (see the photo on the facing page). The radii you mark on the top will vary based on the size of the table base you've made and the rough width and length of your tabletop and leaves. To lay out the curve on the table ends, use the parallel-to-the-rule-joint axis line you made through the top's center point. To lay out the curves for the leaves, use the perpendicular line.

First the table ends: Moving the drywall screw point along the parallel line adjusts the radius of the circle you swing from the tips of the spurs. Setting the screw point closer to the center of the table will make a tighter circle, and if you move it farther away, you will make a wider circle.

Hold the trammel so that the drywall screw sticks in the parallel line and the other end rests on one of the spurs. Swing the pencil end of the trammel in an arc to the spur on the opposite side of the table. Move the screw up and down the parallel line and swing arcs with different radii until you find one that's pleasing to your eye. When you find a radius you like, mark the nonscrew end of the trammel and drill a hole in the stick so that you can pressure-fit a pencil through it. With the pencil through the stick, draw the circumference from the tip of one spur to the tip of the spur on the opposite side of the tabletop. To swing the same arc on the other end of the table, set the screw point the same distance from the tabletop center point in the other direction.

For both table leaves, you are going to swing an arc using the perpendicular-to-the-rule-joint axis line you drew through the center of the tabletop. And this time, instead of swinging an arc from the tips of one of the spurs, you'll swing the arc from the end of the 1½-in. line that's perpendicular to the table-leg line.

The last thing to do in laying out the tabletop is to relieve the corners of the table-end arcs. Relieving the corners adds to the illusion that the top is a true circle. Using a compass, swing a pleasing arc from a point on the table-end arc 1 in. past the line where the leaf meets the top to the point you've marked 1½ in. down the table-leg line.

After cutting out the tabletop with a jigsaw, I planed, scraped, and sanded it until I was blue in the face. I used 340-grit sandpaper to knock the sharp edges off the tabletop and base, wanting to maintain the

TWO TRAMMELS SWING DIFFERENT ARCS. By using different center points, trammels of different lengths and a compass, it's possible to lay out a gracefully curving tabletop of any dimension. The curves break at each corner spur, and the spurs are aligned with the table's legs.

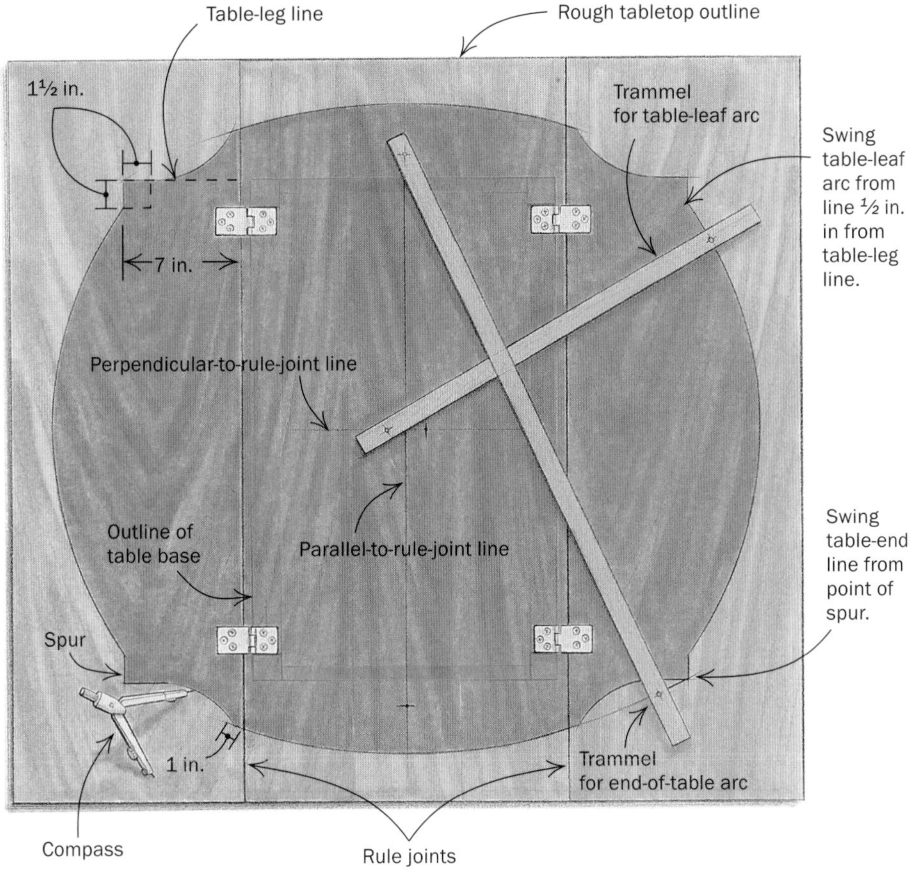

Table-leg line

Rough tabletop outline

1½ in.

Trammel for table-leaf arc

Swing table-leaf arc from line ½ in. in from table-leg line.

7 in.

Perpendicular-to-rule-joint line

Outline of table base

Parallel-to-rule-joint line

Swing table-end line from point of spur.

Spur

1 in.

Trammel for end-of-table arc

Compass

Rule joints

crisp corners. To accommodate the drop-leaf-hinge barrels and to make the tabletop lie flat on the base, I knocked out a small mortise on the base under each barrel. To attach the top to the base, I used small, L-shaped wood buttons that screw to the underside of the top and fit into chiseled slots in the base.

I was going to use an oil-and-shellac finish on the table, but after the first coat of oil, I didn't like the way it looked on the mahogany, so I'll probably scrape it off and go for a straight shellac finish. Hey, we all make mistakes; we all change our minds. Look what happened to my marriage. I just hope that my ex-father-in-law hasn't changed his mind about Pembroke tables.

STEVE LATTA

Federal-Style Oval Inlays

Woodworkers who specialize in 18th-century reproductions tend to be an obsessive bunch. Whether they're turners, carvers, or upholsterers, they find a niche and focus—I mean really focus—on it. For me, it's inlay and marquetry. I could cut all day and every day and still not get enough.

Federal-style furniture originating from the Chesapeake Bay area is full of wonderful details. Late-18th-century Baltimore card tables are a particular favorite of mine. I love their graceful lines, rich bandings, and intricate oval inlays.

Oval inlays tell a lot about a piece of furniture. Just as the styling of ball-and-claw feet suggests a city of origin, inlay patterns also provide clues to a piece's history. The leaf-and-thistle oval shown on the facing page is from a card table made in Baltimore in the early 1800s. Although I've seen this oval on some pieces from Charleston, S.C., only Baltimore cabinet-makers used the style of lower banding around the legs and aprons of this table. This oval appears on numerous tables from the region. I've also seen it adorning the top of a Baltimore sofa, too.

Most cabinetmakers in the 19th century did not make their own ovals. They were purchased from local "stringing" shops or imported from England. Rural shops, without access to manufactured inlays, made their own. These ovals were usually a little more crude in their styling and execution,

but they lent their own personality to a piece as well.

The leaf-and-thistle oval pictured here was copied from a card table containing four ovals in all. One of the ovals was exceptional in design and execution while the other three were comparatively crude. In the context of the whole table, however, they look great. When making ovals, don't fret over every little gap, broken curve, irregularity, and chip. Ovals are accents to a piece, not the primary focus.

PATTERNS MAY BE HARD TO FIND, BUT VENEERS ARE READILY AVAILABLE

Finding accurate patterns of classic ovals can be difficult. One of my favorite source books for photos is *Southern Furniture: 1680–1830, Colonial Williamsburg Collection* by Ronald Hurst and Jonathan Prown (Colonial Williamsburg Foundation, 1998). I also have a friend in the restoration business, and I check with him regularly to see whether something particularly stunning has come through his shop.

Holly and satinwood are the traditional veneers used in ovals, and they are readily available. For the background veneer I use dyed holly, which can be difficult to find. Some mail-order catalogs offer dyed and nondyed veneers (see Sources of Supply on p. 96). Burls, crotches, and other figured woods make wonderful backgrounds as well, and they are readily available.

Two Methods Are Used to Cut This Style of Oval

Although cutting ovals is fun, it can be a little nerve-racking. You have to maintain a smooth, fluid motion. To establish that rhythm, trace some lines onto scrap stock, using a small French curve, then make practice cuts using hand and power saws.

I use two classic marquetry techniques to make this style of oval: stack cutting and bevel cutting (see the drawings on p. 90). In stack cutting, all of the veneers used in the oval are layered one atop another. The upper parts of the oval—flower, stem, and folded leaves—are stack-cut. For reasons of economy, most of the original 18th-century ovals were made this way. Layers could be piled upon each other, allowing the cutter to produce 10 to 15 ovals at a time. But this method produces a gap between elements the width of the sawblade.

Bevel cutting eliminates gaps. Parts fit together like a tapered plug going into a cone-shaped hole. Grain orientation is much easier to control when bevel cutting, and that makes for a more dynamic oval. In this oval, for example, the grain of the large leaves is oriented 45° to the straight-grained, skinny center stems. On the downside, however, bevel cutting doesn't lend itself to mass production. Ovals are made one at a time.

STACK CUTTING GOES QUICKLY BUT LEAVES GAPS

Before beginning an inlay, select the veneer stock, sandwich it between a couple of layers of medium-density fiberboard (MDF) and preshrink it. I place the bundle behind the stove or radiator and let the heat shrink the wood for a few days. Moisture from the hide glue used in assembly will swell the wood back to its original size and reduce gaps between the cutouts. If you don't preshrink the veneers, they'll still swell from the glue but creep back later.

The stack that includes parts 1 to 5 (see the drawing on the facing page) as well as that portion of the background is made up of small rectangles, about 3 in. by 4 in. Place the green background on the bottom and the satinwood, which makes up many small, delicate pieces that are most likely to break, in the middle. The holly goes on top. To make multiple ovals, use a separate piece of veneer for each, keeping like species together. Sandwich the stack between two-ply veneer, which will prevent chipping during cutting. To make the two-ply, glue up pieces of veneer with the grain oriented at 90° to each other.

Next, glue a full-sized photocopy of the pattern to the top of the stack using a spray adhesive such as 3M's Spray Mount™. Outside the borders of the oval, tack the stack together with small brads. Predrill the holes for the brads before nailing. Rigid foam or rigid cardboard make a good nailing backer block. Finally, snip off the points and file or grind the stubs smooth.

To cut the stack I use an old Delta ® scroll saw that I picked up at an auction for $85. It is a beautiful machine that doesn't vibrate. The cutting action is straight up and down. Many scroll saws operate with an orbital motion, which cuts quicker but not as smoothly. I use an electric foot switch, which allows me to keep both hands on the stock while cutting.

In stack cutting, the elements in the foreground are cut first (see the top photo on p. 92). The opposite is true for bevel cuts. Drill a small hole in the middle of the leafy section of the oval and thread a No. 2/0 Eberle or Olson™ blade through it. This hole will be cut away later when the large leaves are cut in. Cut out pieces 1 to 5. The hairiest parts to cut out are the little ones, such as the stem. If the blade binds and dribbles the stack like a basketball, there will be lots of broken pieces that aren't easily repaired. It's easy to get frustrated, so take your time, and don't worry if you stray a bit from the lines.

■ Cutting Methods

STACK CUTTING

Layers of veneer are piled atop one another and sandwiched between two-ply veneer to prevent tearout.

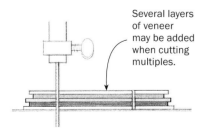

Several layers of veneer may be added when cutting multiples.

Stack cutting results in a gap between elements the thickness of the sawblade.

BEVEL CUTTING

Only matching pairs of stacked parts can be cut at once.

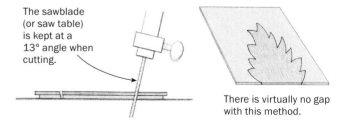

The sawblade (or saw table) is kept at a 13° angle when cutting.

There is virtually no gap with this method.

Both stack cutting and bevel cutting are used to produce this leaf-and-thistle design.

STEP 1

Parts 1 to 5 are stack-cut to form the thistle and folded leaves along with the background.

VENEER SANDWICH. Holly, satinwood, and green-dyed holly are placed between two-ply veneer to prevent tearout.

STEP 2

The leaves, parts 6 to 8, are bevel-cut. Each leaf is then bevel-cut into the background as a unit.

LOOK ALIVE. Leaves are oriented 45° to the veins for a more lifelike look, and sand-shading adds depth.

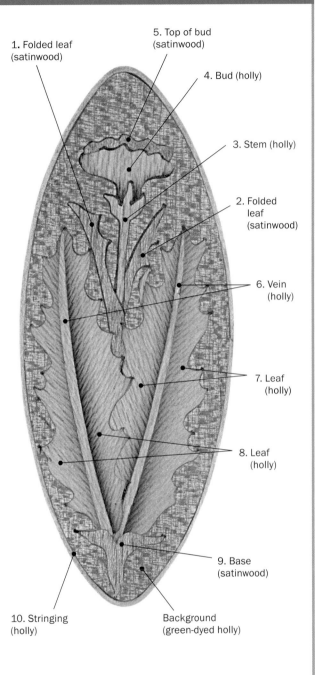

1. Folded leaf (satinwood)

5. Top of bud (satinwood)

4. Bud (holly)

3. Stem (holly)

2. Folded leaf (satinwood)

6. Vein (holly)

7. Leaf (holly)

8. Leaf (holly)

9. Base (satinwood)

10. Stringing (holly)

Background (green-dyed holly)

STEP 3

The base (9) is bevel-cut into the background, the finished piece is cut into an oval, and the stringing (10) is applied.

Stack-Cut the Thistle and Folded Leaves

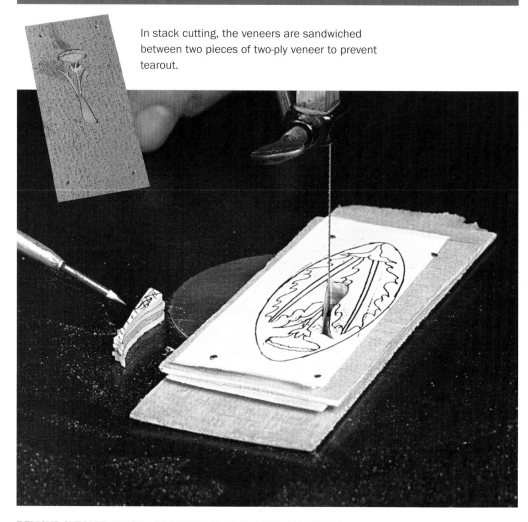

In stack cutting, the veneers are sandwiched between two pieces of two-ply veneer to prevent tearout.

REMOVE CUTOUTS BEFORE PROCEEDING TO THE NEXT ELEMENT. Although only one oval is being cut in this photo, you can stack enough veneers to cut several ovals at once.

USING HIDE GLUE, TACK THE STACK-CUT PARTS ONTO WHITE PAPER. The gaps left by the blade's kerf will be filled later with dark wax, which creates a sharp, thin outline.

GLUING AND CLAMPING. After gluing a piece of onion-skin or tracing paper to the face of the partially completed oval, clamp it between blocks of wood. Veneers come in many thicknesses. To even out the pressure when clamping mixed stock, use strips of newspaper.

After pieces 1 to 5 have been cut, push the nails out of the stack with an awl and free up the background. Dry-fit the parts to the background. Then sand-shade the appropriate parts (for more on sand shading, see the sidebar on p. 97). Place a drop of glue (I use hide glue for marquetry) on the back side of each piece and tack the assembly down to a sheet of white paper (see the bottom left photo on the facing page). Glue a layer of thinner paper, such as onion-skin or tracing paper, over the top or face side of the parts. Place several layers of newspaper over the onion-skin or tracing paper to even out the pressure, and clamp everything between two blocks of wood (see the bottom right photo on the facing page). A sheet of waxed paper placed between the oval and the newspaper will keep things from sticking. At this point, the oval has a flower, a stem, and a pair of folded leaves set into the green background.

THE MORE DIFFICULT SECTIONS ARE BEVEL-CUT

For the next phase, work from the back of the oval and cut all of the parts at a 13-degree angle (see the photos above). When using a scrollsaw, simply tilt the table at the proper angle. When using a fretsaw, support the work with a piece of scrap plywood with a bird's mouth (a slot and a hole) cutout. Bevel back both sides of the slot so that you can hold the saw at about 13 degrees.

To mark the parts from the back side, copy the original drawing using tracing paper. Then flip this tracing over and transfer it to the stock, using a piece of carbon paper and a sharpened dowel as a stylus. I use carbon paper with a white backing, which makes it easier to see the pattern.

Veneer is also stacked in bevel cutting, but the stack consists only of mating pairs of individual components and a piece of backer material. Bevel cutting produces a good fit between parts because the angle of the blade results in the top piece being slightly bigger than the bottom one. When

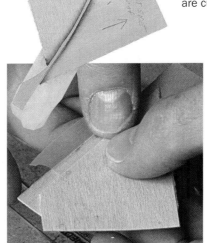

■ Bevel-Cut the Large Leaf Elements

Bevel cutting is more time-consuming because only matching pairs of parts are cut simultaneously.

USING CLEAR TAPE, ATTACH A VEIN TO ONE HALF OF A LEAF. Tilt the scrollsaw's table to about 13°. Cut the first half of the leaf's vein. Bevel cutting will produce a very snug joint between parts.

TAPE THE SECOND LEAF HALF OVER THE VEIN. Veneer tape is used on the face side (not shown) to join the first two pieces together. All cutting and temporary taping is done on the back side (shown). The pencil lines denote grain orientation.

the parts are fitted together, they fall into place without a gap. I angle the bevel in such a way that when the oval is assembled, the inner parts are all wedged in place. That provides a mechanical fit to reinforce the glue bond.

The leaves are the hardest parts to cut because they have sharp, fragile points along the outer edge. Additionally, a vein runs up the middle of each leaf. Begin by cutting rough stock for the leaves. Orient the grain of the leaves 45° to their central vein to make the leaves more lifelike.

The veins and matching inner edges of the leaves are cut first. Take the left half of a leaf and place it atop a straight-grained piece for the center vein. Be sure to leave enough overlap (about ½ in.) on the other side for the other half of the vein. Tape the two pieces using ordinary clear tape. Flip the tracing of the pattern to reveal the back side, then lay it on top of the veneer into proper position so that the vein pattern is centered over the matching piece of veneer. Slip a piece of carbon paper between the tracing and veneer and transfer the line marking the left half of the vein. Cut one side of the vein. Remember to place a piece of scrap veneer between the stock and saw table to reduce tearout.

When done, remove the waste that's taped to one half of the leaf. The leaf and vein should mate snugly. Sand-shade the inner portion of the leaf, then attach it to the vein, using veneer tape. Repeat the process for the other leaf half and vein. All veined leaves are done in this manner.

Next, cut out the leaves (see the photos on the facing page). First, peel and scrape the paper backer tacked onto the back of the oval. Align the tracing, being sure to work from the back side, over the partially completed oval. Then insert a leaf section

and align it. Remember, in bevel cutting, the background elements are cut first. Hold the leaf in place with clear tape. Using carbon paper, trace the outline of the leaf. If necessary, touch up the lines with a pencil.

Now comes the hard part. The thistle leaves have lots of little points, which tend to break off when power sawing. At this point I switch to a fretsaw with a 12-in. throat and a No. 2/0 blade. Because sharp turns are needed when cutting points, I grind the teeth off the bottom inch of the blade using a Dremel™ tool. I grind the blade nearly round so that I can easily pivot the stock about the axis of the blade without catching a tooth.

Drill a small hole at the leaf's base, thread the blade and, using the wooden support with the bird's mouth, cut in the leaf. Keep the blade tilted at about 13°. Align the saw so that the top is at 1 o'clock and the bulk of the leaf is to the left, and cut counterclockwise. Swivel the leaf—not the saw—to maintain a continuous bevel around the perimeter. The direction of feed is critical. Go the other direction, and you end up with big gaps between parts.

When cutting the first leaf, cut a big arc around the region where the two leaves overlap, and leave material behind. Never cut a section twice; the result will be unsightly gaps. After the first leaf has been completed, tape it into place on the oval with veneer tape. Go back to the pattern, align the second leaf and repeat the previous steps. Lastly, cut out the base (part 9).

■ Bevel-Cut the Leaves into the Background

MAKE A TRACING AND FLIP IT OVER. Slip a leaf assembly into position. Using carbon paper, transfer the pattern of the leaves onto the veneer.

CUT CAREFULLY. Keep the fretsaw blade angled at about 13° and cut slowly and steadily, turning the stock as needed. Note the plywood support with a bird's-mouth cutout.

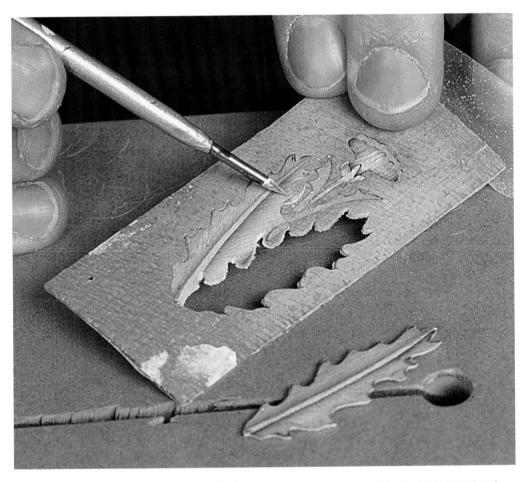

LEAVES FALL INTO PLACE. Once the first leaf has been completed, place it in the background and secure it with veneer tape. Return to the pattern, align the second leaf, and repeat the steps.

A SLIGHTLY DIFFERENT WAY OF MOUNTING THE OVAL

At this point the oval is still a rectangle. Traditionally, the next step would be to border the design with an oval made from stringing, then inlay the finished piece and, finally, remove the paper to see the result. I prefer to see the face side of an oval before committing it to a piece of furniture. So I glue my assembly to a piece of scrap veneer first, then scrape off the paper face and examine it. Barring complications, the oval is ready to size and border.

Trace an outline onto the assembly. For this I made a Plexiglas® oval template (see the left photo below). I cut it out using a scrollsaw, then filed the edges fair.

Slice a piece of stringing from a sheet of holly veneer. To help prevent the holly from breaking while bending it into shape, use a thin feeler gauge and a soldering iron with a heat regulator. Place the stringing on the tip of the iron (don't use too much heat or it will scorch) and wrap the feeler gauge around the wood to hold the bend (see the center photo below). When the tight curves are set, wrap the oval and join the ends in a miter, made with a chisel (see the right photo below). Apply glue to the edge of the oval, wrap the stringing around it, and clamp it with clear tape.

If you've made it this far, setting the oval into solid stock will seem like child's play. Place the oval in the correct position and mark its location with a sharp knife. Use a router to remove the bulk of the waste, then finish up using gouges and chisels.

■ Size and Band the Oval

MARK THE OVAL USING A PLEXIGLAS TEMPLATE. After cutting the oval, file the edges fair.

BEND THE STRINGING USING A SOLDERING IRON SET ON LOW. A feeler gauge helps nudge the stringing into shape. The author modified his soldering iron's tip with different-diameter brass tubes slid inside each other.

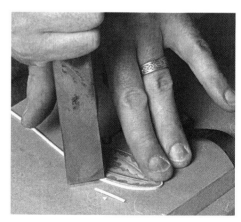

WRAP THE OVAL WITH THE HOLLY. Cut the miter joint using a chisel held vertically. After applying glue, hold the stringing in place with tape.

FINISHING INVOLVES SOME DETAIL WORK

Finishing inlaid pieces can be a bit tricky. I have had some nice work ruined by finishers who improperly prepared the work. It tears my heart out when that happens. Although different pieces may require slightly different procedures, here's one that works well. Give the entire piece a washcoat with a 1-lb. cut of shellac. Then, using a 2½-lb. cut, paint the ovals and the lower stringings. With a small brush, lightly stain the leg, avoiding the ovals, banding, and stringing. Once a rhythm is established, it goes fairly quickly. Follow up with a couple of coats of orange shellac topped off with a dark wax. The dark wax fills gaps in the oval and, like a fine-point pen, highlights the borders between elements.

■ VERY FINE SAND MAKES THE BEST SHADING MEDIUM

I discovered the world-renowned, fine, white-sand beaches of Siesta Key, Fla., when I visited my parents there several years ago. The sand is very different from what you find on most beaches. Siesta Key sand is as fine as granulated sugar, the best kind for sand-shading veneer. Before leaving the Keys I filled two plastic bags with the fine white powder, loaded them in my suitcase and prayed I wouldn't have to explain myself to airport security.

The sand passed through without questions, and I have enough to last many years. If you can't justify a trip to Florida for this mission, check out feed and grain stores, flower shops, or pet shops for fine sand. Avoid large, coarse sand, which will make it difficult to sand-shade small parts without burning.

Sand shading takes a little practice. I use an electric hot plate and a cast-iron skillet, which provide controlled, even heat. Spread the sand in uneven piles across the skillet, as shown in the photo above. The shallow piles will scorch veneer quicker than the taller ones. Mold the sand into the shape of the part to be shaded (see the photo at right). Shade smaller pieces by dipping them in a spoonful of hot sand. If a small part falls into the spoon, you will be able to retrieve it without burning yourself and the part. I've burned many a piece into oblivion after losing it in a deep pile of sand.

After scorching, sand the area lightly with 220-grit paper. This will provide a more accurate picture of what the burn will look like after finishing.

CONTROLLED HEAT. Heat the sand in an iron skillet atop a hot plate. Spread the sand in uneven piles across the skillet.

MOUND, THEN DIP. Mold the sand into the shape of the piece. Dip the part for a few seconds at a time, checking it frequently.

RANDALL O'DONNELL

Curly Cherry Highboy (Part I)

When I watch a sawyer cut open a hardwood log that has highly figured wood inside, it's like stumbling across a buried treasure. Wood like that is a gift of nature, and it deserves the best showcase I can provide.

Most of the pieces that I make are reproductions of Early American furniture, and for showing off unusually beautiful lumber, there's nothing quite like a high chest of drawers. Unlike a tabletop, a highboy can be appreciated from a distance, and the character of the wood really becomes three-dimensional. Add a bonnet top with a dramatic gooseneck molding, brasses, and carved fans and finials—all dancing on cabriole legs—and the result is a piece of furniture with real presence.

I've examined a number of original highboys. Only a few stand out as true masterpieces, but many include wonderful details that provide a rich palette for the period furniture maker. This piece is my interpretation of a Massachusetts style from about 1750. The blocked apron, finials, arch cutouts, and shells are based on designs from Boston in that era.

The highboy exercises just about every skill of the traditional cabinetmaker: turning, sculpting, mortise-and-tenon joinery, dovetailing, carving, and (gasp!) even driving nails where appropriate. Colonial cabinetmakers usually had apprentices handle routine tasks. As an independent craftsman, my apprentices are machines that prepare stock quickly so that I can devote my time

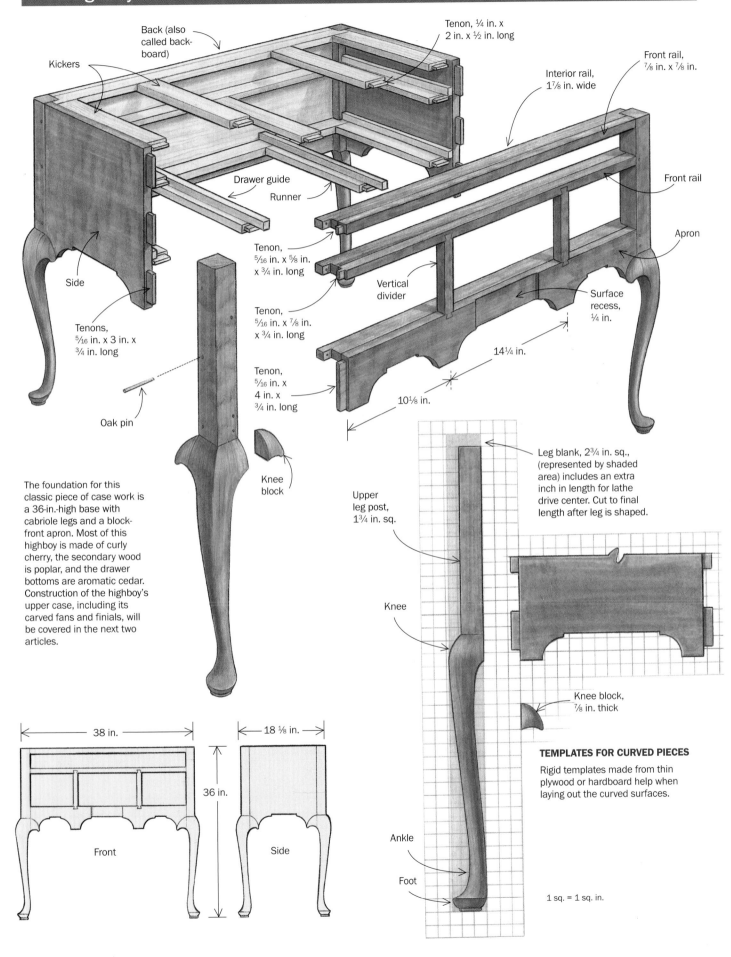

Back (also called back-board)

Kickers

Tenon, ¼ in. x 2 in. x ½ in. long

Interior rail, 1⅞ in. wide

Front rail, ⅞ in. x ⅞ in.

Front rail

Apron

Side

Tenons, 5/16 in. x 3 in. x ¾ in. long

Drawer guide

Runner

Tenon, 5/16 in. x ⅝ in. x ¾ in. long

Vertical divider

Surface recess, ¼ in.

Tenon, 5/16 in. x ⅞ in. x ¾ in. long

14¼ in.

Oak pin

Tenon, 5/16 in. x 4 in. x ¾ in. long

10⅛ in.

Knee block

The foundation for this classic piece of case work is a 36-in.-high base with cabriole legs and a block-front apron. Most of this highboy is made of curly cherry, the secondary wood is poplar, and the drawer bottoms are aromatic cedar. Construction of the highboy's upper case, including its carved fans and finials, will be covered in the next two articles.

Upper leg post, 1¾ in. sq.

Knee

Leg blank, 2¾ in. sq., (represented by shaded area) includes an extra inch in length for lathe drive center. Cut to final length after leg is shaped.

Knee block, ⅞ in. thick

TEMPLATES FOR CURVED PIECES

Rigid templates made from thin plywood or hardboard help when laying out the curved surfaces.

Ankle

Foot

38 in.

18⅛ in.

36 in.

Front

Side

1 sq. = 1 sq. in.

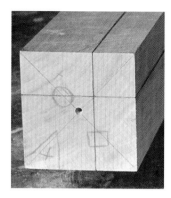

RUN THE GROWTH RINGS DIAGONALLY from the inside corner to the outside corner when laying out the legs. With this orientation, the grain flows with the cabriole curve.

to the critical hand skills that set this piece apart from factory-made furniture. Fine carving, hand-cut dovetails, and handplaned surfaces remove any trace of the machines that did the grunt work before me. Economic reality has taught me that even though I can replicate a period piece of furniture, I can't slavishly follow every method of the Colonial makers.

Building this highboy is well within the abilities of the serious amateur cabinetmaker. (This article deals with the lower case. In the next two articles, we'll build the rest of the highboy.) Although it may appear daunting, much of the work amounts to executing just a few traditional joinery techniques over and over. With so many pieces to cut and assemble (see the drawing on p. 99), organization is as important as technique.

SELECT STOCK CAREFULLY

All the curly cherry flat stock needs to finish out at ⅞ in. thick, so I usually start with roughsawn, 1⅛-in. stock. The gooseneck molding and lower finials are made from 8/4 curly cherry stock, and I use sound I 2/4 straight-grained stock for the legs and the top finials.

All secondary wood is poplar, except drawer bottoms. All internal frame parts are ⅞-in.-thick stock to match the cherry. Drawer sides and backs are ⅝-in.-thick poplar, back boards are ½ in. thick and drawer bottoms are ⅜-in. aromatic cedar.

Before cutting any wood, select the best figured stock for the most prominent areas: the drawer fronts, the front apron, and the wide scroll board at the top of the upper

DON'T CUT THE WASTE COMPLETELY FREE OF THE BLANK. Leave a small connecting bridge so waste pieces don't need to be taped or nailed back into place when the stock is rotated to saw the other face.

ONLY THE FOOT IS TURNED. With the leg still mounted in the lathe, shape it with a spokeshave and rasp.

case. Careful stock selection provides a kind of visual rhythm to the piece, uniting upper and lower cases. If I can, I use boards from the same log.

START BY SHAPING THE LEGS

Even when empty, this is a heavy piece of furniture. Leg strength is important. That's why I look for sound, straight-grained stock to rip into 2¾-in.-sq. leg blanks. Make the blanks an inch longer at the upper end so the lathe drive center has material to bite into. This extra inch of stock will be cut off later, after the leg is shaped and mortised. When laying out the leg profile, align the blanks so the annual rings run diagonally from the inside corner to the outside corner (see the top photo on the facing page). This makes the strongest possible leg as well as the most attractive one. The grain lines flow with the contour of the cabriole shape.

First make a full-sized template of the cabriole leg profile on thin plywood or hardboard. Using this template, mark out the leg profile on all four blanks. Before bandsawing the cabriole profile, I define the shoulder line at the junction of the upper post and the curve of the knee. All I do is crosscut the two outside faces of each leg on the tablesaw to a depth just shy of the finished surface.

Careful bandsawing makes sculpting the leg much easier. When bandsawing the cabriole profile, I don't saw off the waste completely. Instead, I leave a small, connecting bridge between the leg and the waste. This gives the leg good support as I make the cuts on each face of the leg (see the bottom photo on the facing page). Finally, I return to the first face and cut through the remaining bridged segments. This bridging method ensures perfect alignment of the sawn faces with the template and eliminates the fussy process of reattaching the sawn waste in some other way to make all the cuts.

Once the leg is sawn to rough shape, mark the centers on both ends of the blank, and turn the foot on the lathe. Be sure to make a crisp top edge on the foot (see the photo above). This gives a nice reference edge from which to rasp and file the shape.

From this point, I shape the rest of the cabriole profile by hand, using the lathe as a vise to hold the stock. I start with a spokeshave to remove a lot of waste quickly. For shaping, though, a pattern maker's rasp gives the best results. Finally, I use files and sandpaper to finish the curved leg and foot. Leave edges at the knees sharp, and be careful not to round over any edges where the knee blocks will be attached.

MORTISE THE LEG POSTS

At this point, the upper part of the leg has been laid out but is still 2¾ in. sq. This is when I lay out and cut the mortises for the back, sides, and all three front rails. The full width of the leg stock and the extra inch of

A PLUNGE ROUTER WITH A SPIRAL BIT ROUGHS OUT THE MORTISES. The full stock width of the blank provides support for the router.

AFTER THE ROUTER, USE A CHISEL to pare and square the mortises to the scribed lines.

length provide stable support for the router (see the top photo). I use a plunge router fitted with a spiral up-cut bit. The bit diameter is slightly smaller than the finished mortise width so that I can shave the cut exactly to my scribed lines. After plunging the mortises, pare to the layout lines, and square up the inside corners with a chisel.

Once all the mortises are cut, rip and crosscut the upper leg posts to size. Stay outside the layout line by about ¹⁄₁₆ in. The excess will be planed flush with the sides after assembly. Also, be sure to mark and save the waste pieces from the upper part of the legs. These pieces will be used for making the knee blocks and will give the best possible grain match with the leg.

PREPARE THE STOCK FOR THE CARCASE

Loggers in my area call me when they find an exceptional tree—one that is big, straight and, if I'm lucky, figured. I have to act fast, though, because it's always a race against the veneer-log buyers who also want dazzling wood. Midway through this project, I had to drop everything and dash off to the woods to check out a tip. But that's how I get the figured wood I need for my furniture.

Start by sawing the rough wood so that it's a few inches longer than needed and about ½ in. wider. Normally, I'd surface one face and true up one edge on the jointer and move to the thickness planer. Highly figured wood like this, though, is prone to tearout, so I do the final thicknessing on a wide-belt sander. Later, I'll handplane and scrape all the parts to clean up the fuzzy sanded surface and get the silky, hand-worked texture that's so essential to period furniture. Tool marks reveal an intimacy between wood and maker. But to me, it really doesn't matter whether the stock initially was thicknessed by a power planer or with scrub and jack planes.

CUT OUT THE FRONT RAILS, SIDES, AND BACK

Three tenons connect each case side and the back with the legs, making for some 17 in. of cross-grain construction. With seasonal humidity changes, there's a strong possibility of a crack developing in the sides or the back. None of my furniture has developed any cracks, but it is quite common on original pieces. Because a crack along the grain of a side or back doesn't affect structural integrity and gives a look of authenticity, I don't worry about it.

With stock for the sides and back cut to their finished width and length, I use the router and edge guide to start the tenons by cutting a long tongue in each end of the sides and back.

Next lay out and cut the individual tenons with the bandsaw, and then use a chisel to pare the ragged bandsaw cuts to the shoulder lines. Don't cut the bottom scroll yet. Wait until the joints have been dry-fit.

The three horizontal front rails (including the apron) are cut from a single board. Mark the stock to keep the rails in sequence. For these parts, it's easier to lay out and cut the tenons first before ripping the stock into individual rails.

Sides, back, and rails should be test-fitted to the legs. If all fits well, take the case apart. Using full-sized patterns, lay out the scroll on the bottom edge of the apron, sides and back. Bandsaw to shape, and clean up the sawn surfaces with a spokeshave and rasp.

The center area on the apron is recessed (or blocked) to align with the fan carving on the drawer above it. Remove the bulk of the waste in this area with the bandsaw, and then finish with a rasp and scraper. Drill the two ½-in.-dia. holes in the bottom of the apron for the turned tenons of the drop finials.

The two vertical dividers between the three lower drawers are milled to size and a dovetail cut on each end. The divider is ⅞ in. deep, but the dovetail only extends ½ in. deep. Fit these pieces to the middle rail and apron after the front legs and rails are glued up.

MAKE THE INTERIOR FRAMING MEMBERS

Along with the parts already made, the case needs additional framing to reinforce joints and support the drawers. The next step is to cut stock for the drawer runners and kickers. Collect all of these pieces, and cut the tenons on the ends at one time (see the photos at right).

Leg post-to-rail joint strength is my chief concern, so I reinforce this area with interior rails that are notched around the inside corners of the posts. These pieces are glued to both the front rails and the back of the case.

There are three pairs of interior rails. The front interior rails are made of cherry to match the front rails. The back rails are made of poplar. With the exception of the wood species, they are identical. Group the rail pairs. Lay out and cut all the mortises first, and then fit the tenons.

CUTTING TENONS BY THE BATCH SAVES TIME. Clamping the runners and kickers together also makes it easier to keep tenons uniform.

MARK THE SHOULDER LINE on the narrow edge of each tenon. Cut the waste away on the bandsaw.

Assemble the Base in Three Stages

A sure way to induce a panic attack is by trying to glue all the parts at once. Having a bunch of glue-slathered parts dripping everywhere is bad enough, but with so many parts to handle, glue can start to set before all the joints are seated and the case squared up. So I begin with just the front

PLANE THE UPPER LEG POSTS FLUSH WITH THE FRONT. A file, chisel, and scraper help to bring all the leg posts flush with the front, sides, and back.

INTERIOR RAILS GLUED TO THE FRONT RAILS and back board reinforce the case and permit longer tenons to be used on drawer runners and kickers.

assembly. Glue up the two front legs and the three front rails. Be sure to check that the assembly remains square after the clamps are in place.

After the glue has cured, use a jointer plane, chisel, and a rasp to fair the leg posts flush with the rails (see the photo at left). Now position the two vertical dividers over the middle rail and apron, and scribe and cut the dovetails. The dividers can now be glued into place.

The backboard is glued up with the back legs, clamped and allowed to dry. Once the back assembly has been removed from the clamps, fair the back leg posts flush with the back.

Once you've glued the interior rails on the front and back assemblies (see the photo below), dry-fit the sides and all the drawer runners and kickers (see the top photo on the facing page). If everything fits well, apply glue to all the mortises and tenons, and bring the whole assembly together and clamp. This operation may take extra hands. Two people certainly make the assembly less nerve-racking.

Be sure the case remains square after the clamps are tightened. After the glue has dried, clean up any glue squeeze-out, then fair the leg posts flush with the case sides.

Now install drawer-side guides, which prevent the drawers from cocking when pushed into place. The guides are pieces of poplar, glued and nailed (as was done on the originals) to the runners.

Attach the Knee Blocks

Knee blocks provide a graceful transition between the legs and neighboring surfaces. You'll need six blocks: two each on the three sides that show. Using a template, lay out the profile on leg-post offcuts. Bandsaw the block profile, dress surfaces that butt against the leg and side or apron, and rough shape the curve. Now glue the knee blocks in place (see the bottom left photo on the facing page). Clamping pressure must

Dry-fit all parts to find potential problems before glue is applied.

GLUE THE ROUGH-SHAPED KNEE BLOCKS IN PLACE. After the glue dries, use chisels, rasps, and sandpaper to blend the entire knee.

squeeze the knee block into the flat on the leg blank and the apron and side. After the glue has dried, fair the entire knee area with carving tools, rasps, files, and sandpaper. Some excess wood still must be removed on the inside curve of all four legs so that they'll blend with the apron scroll.

FIT THE TENON PINS

After sanding the case, drill holes in the leg posts for the tenon pins. They should be made of riven (split) oak. A riven pin is less likely to split or break. Spokeshave the pin with a slight taper to give a tight fit. Before driving them into place, test-fit the pins in a scrap block. Cut these pins slightly proud of the surface using a piece of sandpaper as a gauge, and peen the ends to give an aged look.

NEXT ARTICLE: THE UPPER CASE With the lower case complete, the next step is building the graceful upper cabinet that crowns this highboy.

RANDALL O'DONNELL

Curly Cherry Highboy (Part II)

AN AMERICAN CLASSIC—
The dovetailed upper case of this bonnet-top highboy is capped by a sweeping gooseneck molding, which is made with hand and power tools. Construction of the lower case was covered in the previous article.

Earlier in my career, I built kitchen cabinets. At that time, dovetailing meant using a jig and router. I dovetailed more than a thousand drawers that way. But when I decided to become a period furniture maker, I knew those days were over—only hand-cut dovetails would do. Abandoning the speed of a jig for tedious handwork seemed crazy at first, but with my first hand-cut joint, I learned it wasn't as hard as I thought.

Dovetail joinery is a large part of what goes into constructing the upper case of this highboy. With its bonnet top and graceful moldings, this chest of drawers appears to be a formidable project. But stripped of embellishment, it's simply a large dovetailed box containing smaller dovetailed boxes.

Finding high-quality, wide stock was my biggest challenge. I was fortunate to find outstanding curly cherry. I used poplar for all the secondary wood except the drawer bottoms, where I used aromatic cedar. Using cedar is more work because it involves joining narrow stock, but the wonderful smell that escapes as you open a drawer makes the effort worthwhile. (I later learned that cedar causes finish deterioration in an enclosed case—assuming the inside of the case is sealed and finished. Now, I use pine drawer bottoms in upper cases but still offer cedar bottoms in the base because it is open to circulation.)

I described my approach for building the base unit in the article on pp. 98–104. Now

I'll detail construction of the upper case. That involves making the carcase, framing the bonnet top, making the drawers, and carving the curved crown, or gooseneck, molding.

BUILDING THE BASIC BOX

It's virtually impossible to find a single board of figured wood wide enough for the sides. But two well-matched boards glued together look fine. The first step is to glue up stock for the case top, bottom, and sides. A piece of furniture like this needs stock that's slightly thicker than what's usually used on case pieces. I use ⅞-in.-thick stock for the entire case, internal framing, and drawer fronts.

I start by flattening one face and jointing one edge of each board. Then I thickness plane the boards to within ¹⁄₁₆ in. of their final thickness. Next, on the tablesaw, I rip the boards to width. I usually don't bother to joint the boards after ripping because I've found that with a good blade and a true-running saw arbor, it's not necessary.

Now I glue up the boards. Once the glue has dried, I sand the pieces to thickness on a wide belt sander. Later, after all the joinery has been cut, I'll surface all the sides, inside and out, with a handplane and cabinet scraper. This gives a handworked texture.

The case is joined at the corners with through dovetails (see the sidebar on p. 108). The top corners are hidden by the moldings and bonnet, and the bottom corners are covered by the base and the waist mold-

ing. This doesn't mean you should be less careful in the joinery, but it does relieve some of the pressure. Flat and square boards make dovetailing easier.

After cutting the dovetails on all four corners, I lay the sides on the bench so I can mark the location of the dadoes that will house the drawer runners (see the drawings below). Using a router, I cut ⅞-in.-wide by ⅛-in.-deep dadoes across the width of the sides.

A rabbet runs around the back inside edge of the case to house the back boards. Using a router, I rabbet the top and bottom pieces across their entire length. The rabbet on each side piece, though, is stopped so that it doesn't break through the outside of the case. Rounded corners can be squared up with a chisel.

The last thing to do on the case is prepare it for the scroll board, the decorated piece at the top of the case. With a router, cut the slots in the top front inside faces of the sides to house the scroll-board tenons. The front edge of the top must be ripped to its finished width to allow the scroll board to slide into place.

INSTALLING RUNNERS AND RAILS

With the bulk of the joinery on the case sides completed, it's time to make the interior framework. Five rails run horizontally across the case at the front and back. These pieces, which help hold the case sides together, are the horizontal dividers between the drawers.

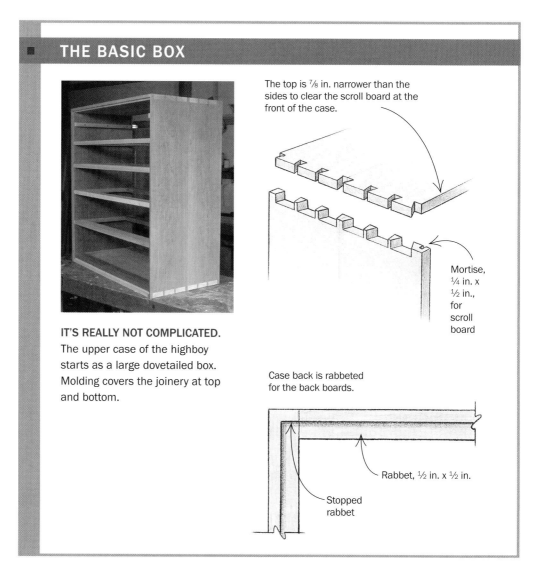

■ THE BASIC BOX

IT'S REALLY NOT COMPLICATED.
The upper case of the highboy starts as a large dovetailed box. Molding covers the joinery at top and bottom.

The top is ⅞ in. narrower than the sides to clear the scroll board at the front of the case.

Mortise, ¼ in. x ½ in., for scroll board

Case back is rabbeted for the back boards.

Rabbet, ½ in. x ½ in.

Stopped rabbet

The highboy uses simple dovetail and mortise-and-tenon joinery. This exploded view identifies all the parts used in this part of the highboy.

46¼ in.

36¼ in.

36 in.

17⅛ in.

RAIL AND RUNNER JOINERY

1 in.

Dado, ⅛ in.

Rails dovetail into the case sides.

Tenon, ¼ in. by ⅞ in. wide, ½ in. long

W1180D.B3.eps-2

Runners are housed in dadoes in the case sides. The ends of the runners tenon into the rails.

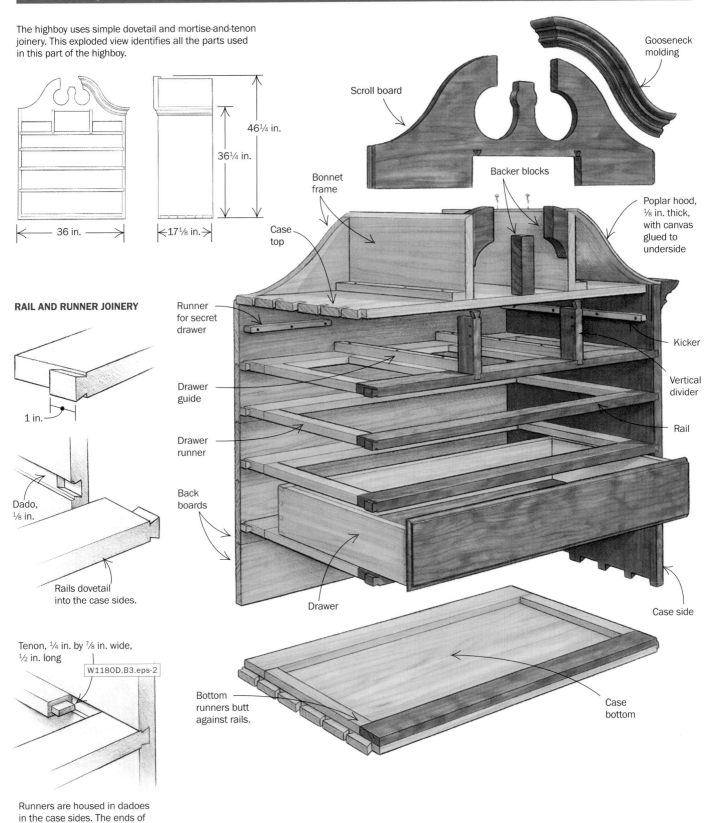

Gooseneck molding

Scroll board

Backer blocks

Poplar hood, ⅛ in. thick, with canvas glued to underside

Bonnet frame

Case top

Runner for secret drawer

Kicker

Drawer guide

Vertical divider

Drawer runner

Rail

Back boards

Drawer

Case side

Bottom runners butt against rails.

Case bottom

It would be easier to cut the front rails out of ⅞-in.-thick flatsawn cherry, but this would put the edge grain on the front of the chest between the drawers. I prefer the look of face grain on the front rails because it complements the grain on the drawer fronts. To get face grain on the front rails, I cut the rails from quartersawn stock. An alternative method is to cut the rails out of 12/4 flatsawn stock, but quartersawn stock is more economical.

I start by ripping the rails to 2¾ in. wide, then cutting them to length. I group the rails into front-and-back pairs and lay out the ¼-in.-wide, ⅞-in.-long mortises that will accept the tenons on the ends of the runners. I use a plunge router with a spiral, up-cut bit to cut the mortises ½ in. deep, then I square up the corners with a chisel.

In the ends of the upper four rail pairs, I make 1-in.-deep dovetails. They'll slide into dovetail sockets that I'll cut after the case is assembled. The bottom rail doesn't need to be held in place by joinery. The rail is simply glued to the case bottom.

The runners, which complete the interior framing, are tenoned into the rails. I group all these parts together and cut the tenons in one setup. (For more on this, see pp. 98–105.)

DRY-FIT THE CASE BEFORE GLUING

Before applying glue, it's best to dry-fit the case members. Any problems should be corrected now. When the pieces fit correctly, I glue up the box, and then I make sure that the case is square.

After the clamps have been removed, I slide the rails into their respective locations and scribe the dovetails into the case sides. With the case on its back, I chop the dovetail sockets for each front rail. Then I place the case face down and chop the rear dovetail sockets. I can now glue the front rails in place and allow the glue to set. Next I lay the case face down, glue the drawer runners into the front rails, and apply glue to just the front 2 in. of the runner in the dado in the case sides. I don't glue the runners to the back rails, so the case sides can expand

and contract freely with humidity changes. Now I glue the back rails in place. And finally, I glue the bottom drawer rail to the case bottom.

The drawer kickers behind the scroll board prevent the top outside drawers from tipping when they are pulled out. Because these kickers do not carry much weight, they are glued and nailed to the interior case sides with cut nails, as was done on many Early American pieces. Because of the cross-grain construction, I apply glue only along the front half of the kicker.

SCROLL BOARD COMPLETES THE CASE WORK

The scroll board is cut from stock that is 14¼ in. wide. Although a single, full-width board is nice, you can join two narrower boards. For the best appearance, though, one of the boards should be at least 11¾ in. wide so that the glue joint is hidden by the gooseneck molding. Before cutting the stock, I make a full-size pattern of the scroll board from thin plywood (see the drawing on the facing page).

It's easier to cut the tenons on the ends of the scroll board and make the center drawer opening while the board is rectangular. I cut the tenons with a router and a spiral bit and edge guide. Then I bandsaw the rough opening for the center drawer.

I use a router fitted with a flush-trimming bit and a template to make the finish opening, and I clean out the two corners with a chisel. I bandsaw the profile at the top of the scroll board, then smooth it on my belt sander.

With the scroll cut, I lay out and carve the circular fan in the plinth (carving for this highboy will be explained in the next article). Once the glue is applied to the tenons, the scroll board can be slid into place (see the top left photo on the facing page).

The next step is to fit the vertical dividers for the top center drawer opening. I cut the dividers to size and dovetail the ends first. Although the divider is 2¾ in. deep, the dovetail is only ½ in. deep. I scribe the dovetails to the rail and scroll board (see the top right photo on the facing page), cut the

Fitting the Scroll Board

SLIDE SCROLL BOARD INTO PLACE. Make sure that the bottom edge is parallel with the rail below.

LAY OUT VERTICAL DIVIDERS. Scribe the dovetails in the ends of the dividers into the scroll board and rail.

Scroll-Board Pattern

To lay out the scroll board, use the grid pattern to make a full-size template on thin plywood.

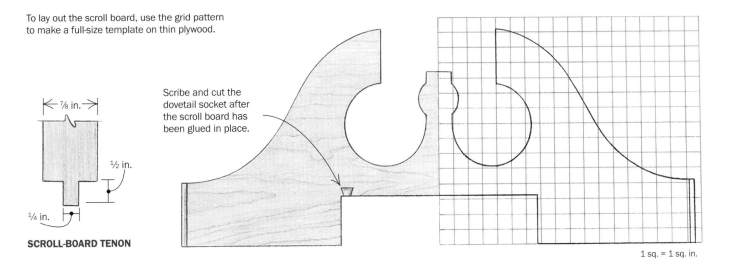

⅞ in.

½ in.

¼ in.

SCROLL-BOARD TENON

Scribe and cut the dovetail socket after the scroll board has been glued in place.

1 sq. = 1 sq. in.

dovetails with a fine backsaw and chisels, and glue the dividers into place.

Riven oak pins anchor the inner edge of the scroll board to the dividers. I drill two ¼-in. holes through each divider and into the edge of the scroll board. I put a little glue on the edge of the pins and drive the pins into the holes, cutting any bit of pro-truding pin flush with the surface. The upper carcase is now ready for the bonnet framework and thin bonnet top and the gooseneck molding.

■ Making the Bonnet

TRACE THE CURVE of the scroll board onto stock for the rear framing member.

HOLD THE BONNET FRAME SQUARE, and drill pilot holes for screws. Once the glue has dried, screws are replaced with forged nails.

SCRIBE THE CURVE ON THE CENTER WALL using the scroll-board template.

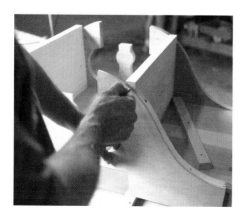

FAIR THE CENTER WALLS TO THE SCROLL CURVE. Using a handplane, the author works from front to rear to prevent chipping the scroll board.

FRAMING THE BONNET

The scroll board establishes the curve of the bonnet, but additional framing is needed to enclose this area and support the hood. The first step is to copy the curve from the front scroll board (see the top left photo below) and to cut the two poplar pieces to shape. Next I cut the stock for the center walls and the cleats that will attach the frame to the case top, and then I glue these pieces together.

I use screws to clamp the parts together temporarily (see the left center photo on the facing page). I replace the screws later with forged nails. The bonnet's frame, like many other traditionally made pieces, does have some cross-grain construction. The nails accommodate the wood's seasonal movement without sacrificing strength.

After the glue has dried, I use my hand-plane to fair the center walls with the curve of the scroll board (see the right photo on the facing page).

GOOSENECK MOLDING IS ROUTED AND THEN CARVED

This traditional molding profile has an astragal bead that stands proud of a large cove, creating a dramatic shadow line. I've made a variety of architectural moldings on my shaper, but this profile, with its S-curve shape, is best worked by a combination of router and carving tools.

I start with a full-size pattern to lay out the S curve on a wide piece of 1½-in.-thick stock. Then I bandsaw and smooth the inside curve to the layout line. I had a pair of router bits made to remove the bulk of the waste quickly (see the left center photo at right). The pilot bearing of the first bit follows the inside curve of the blank (see the top photo) and creates part of the profile (see the drawings at right). The pilot bearing of the second bit follows the shoulder cut made by the first bit and removes more material.

REMOVING WASTE QUICKLY— A router does the heavy work quickly. The author will hand-carve the details in this traditional deep molding.

CUSTOM-MADE ROUTER BITS establish the overall profile of the gooseneck molding.

USE A GOUGE THAT MATCHES THE COVE RADIUS. The router-cut blank leaves guide marks for the width and depth of the cove.

■ Molding in Three Steps

STEP 1

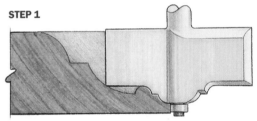

Stock removed by first bit.

STEP 2

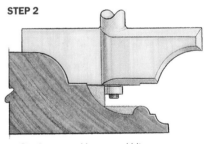

Stock removed by second bit.

STEP 3

Shape with gouges.

◼ Shaping the Gooseneck Molding

CLAMP THE MOLDING IN PLACE, and scribe the miter locations.

SCREWS HOLD THE MOLDING TO THE FENCE so that the molding can be accurately and safely mitered.

LOCATE THE MOLDING ¼ in. above scroll board.

TEST-BEND THE HOOD OVER THE FRAME. To control cracking, glue canvas to the inside of the hood before it's nailed to the bonnet frame.

The remaining material is removed with carving tools, and the entire molding profile is lightly sanded. Finally, I bandsaw the outside curve to separate the molding from the blank and sand the curve to the layout line. The straight moldings for the case sides are made in the same manner.

MOUNT THE MOLDING, AND INSTALL THE HOOD

The top edge of the molding extends about ¼ in. above the scroll board curve to form a rabbet for the front edge of the hood. To locate the miters, I clamp the molding stock in place and scribe the inner edge of the miter.

Mitering the curved molding can be tricky. To hold it in place securely, I screw the molding to the wooden fence on my miter saw. The straight molding is cut by placing the stock upside down with the back edge against the fence. Once the molding is cut, I drill holes and nail it into place with forged finish nails. The plinth and the upper arch of each scroll have fragile short-grain sections that need reinforcement, so I glue backer blocks behind each of them.

The hood is an 18½-in.-wide poplar board that I plane to ⅛ in. thick. It is bent over the frame and nailed in place (see the bottom right photo). Most antique hoods have cracks in this thin piece of wood, and a few minor splits are unavoidable. But to prevent major cracks, I glue canvas to the underside of the hood with contact cement. This makes a ply construction, and so far, none of my bonnets have any serious cracks. Minor cracks seem to be confined to the ends.

ON THE HOME STRETCH WITH DRAWERS, BACKBOARDS

Once the top and bottom cases have been assembled, I make the drawers. After I select the most highly figured boards for the drawer fronts, I make sure that the growth rings on the stock of all the drawers have the same orientation (the faces closest to the bark are all in or all out). Don't mix them up because I've found that the sap-

MAKE THE DRAWERS after the case work is completed. Batch like parts to speed up the work and produce more consistent results.

SECRET DRAWERS ADD A LITTLE MYSTERY. The drawers slide toward the center and can be withdrawn from the case.

wood side will never darken quite as much as the heart, even when the wood comes from the same log.

I cut all the drawer fronts to size, run a bead around the entire drawer front and rabbet the top and sides for a lip—there's no lip on the bottom edge. I check the fit of each drawer and make adjustments. Prior to cutting the dovetails, I carve the fans on the two middle drawer fronts.

Batch all the drawer parts, and lay out and cut the dovetails. The cedar bottoms are fitted after drawers have been glued up. During glue-up, I use a temporary plywood bottom with corners cut off to help square the drawer and to make it easier to clean glue out of the corners.

Even though each drawer front has been fitted to its openings, I work each drawer lightly with a handplane after assembly. A little fussing is usually all that is needed to make each drawer fit perfectly.

Secret compartments add an air of mystery, and this highboy has several. I added two secret drawers inside the case above the two small drawers at the top; they're hidden behind the scroll board. Though not deep, the drawers are plenty big enough for jewelry or documents (see the top right photo). I also made false bottoms in two other drawers. These have a ½-in. space between two drawer bottoms. The upper bottom is completely housed in a groove. The lower bottom slides in from the back. It's held with a loose-fitting nail that can be pulled out with your fingers.

Five individual boards are used to close the back of the case. The ½-in.-thick boards are handplaned inside and out and have tongue-and-groove edges. I fit the boards horizontally across the case and nail them at the ends.

NEXT ARTICLE: THE FANS AND FINIALS. In the next article, Randall O'Donnell describes the carved fans and flame finials that complete this highboy.

RANDALL O'DONNELL

Curly Cherry Highboy (Part III)

magine moving your household and three days later, packing up and moving again. That's what it's like to be an exhibitor at a furniture show. Setting up a booth is hard work. After the carpet was down and everything in place at a recent show, I caught my breath and watched as prospective customers walked into my booth to take a closer look at this highboy. It's almost 7½ ft. tall, and the figure of the curly cherry is exceptional.

Invariably, admirers would walk up to the highboy and somewhat tentatively run their fingers over the fans carved into the two center drawers. Carving seems to serve as the touchstone of a piece. If the carvings look and feel right, customers stay to ask questions, take a brochure and, perhaps, place an order.

I make 18th-century-style furniture. Working within this form, I like to play with the details—to put my stamp on a piece. And nowhere is the ground more fertile for expressing individuality than in carving. Although I have no reservations about using machines for preparing stock, carving is one of several things that I do completely by hand.

In the last two articles, I described building the base and upper case of the highboy. Now it's time to carve the fans in the two center drawers and turn and carve the flame finials that crown the bonnet.

This highboy also has two smaller drop finials in the base and a small, round fan carved in the center of the pediment. These parts use the same carving and turning techniques and are shown in the drawings on p. 124.

Lay Out the Fans with a Compass and Coins

The fans (or shells) in the center of the upper chest and lower base are one of the most eye-catching details on a highboy. There are many regional variations. I adapted these fans from several Boston pieces.

To lay out a fan, I start by drawing a vertical centerline on the drawer front and then marking the horizontal baseline by eye (see the drawing on the facing page). The intersection of these two lines forms the center point of the fan. From this point, I scribe the outer radius, inner radius, and hub diameter with a compass. These lines establish the overall size of the fan.

The fans are sized in proportion to drawer height, and each of these drawer fans has 20 rays. I found that the edge of a coin works well for laying out the ray spacing and scalloped edge. Starting at the center, I lay the coin on one side of the vertical centerline so that the coin just touches the inner radius (see photo 1 on p. 120). I trace a semicircle around the coin, stopping at the outer radius.

I continue scribing the semicircles along the length of the arc and then repeat the procedure on the other half of the fan. I use a penny for the upper drawer fan and a nickel for the lower fan. With the spacing established, I draw lines from the center point to the scallops, marking the rays.

Because the lipped drawers stand proud of the case, the fan carving needs a transition to the horizontal rail below the drawer. To do that, I lower the surface of the drawer front immediately below the fan. I complete the layout by setting the drawer front in the case and scribing a line on the lower edge of the drawer, using the rail as a guide (see photo 2 on p. 120).

Carve the Background and Then the Rays

A crisp scalloped edge heightens the contrast between the fan and drawer surface. To prevent wood splintering beyond the area being worked, I cut the outline of the hub and scallops into the drawer face with carving tools (see photo 3 on p. 120). Using a gouge with a sweep that closely matches the curve makes this easy.

The area on which the rays are carved is worked with gouges to form a shallow S profile. This S contour makes the finished fan sensuous. The serpentine effect can be further accentuated by the depth of the individual rays, so don't hog out too much material at this stage. I get the best results by removing the waste in a series of cuts along the curve. This is mostly cross-grain and skew-cutting (see photo 4 on p. 120), which minimizes the chance of taking too much material at once.

Once the bulk of the waste is removed, I smooth the surface with a sculptor's rasp (see photo 5 on p. 120). I don't use sandpaper until all carving is completed, because grit particles left behind can quickly dull carving tools. Working the surface to the serpentine shape removes most of the ray lines between the hub and the inner radius. Now I redraw them.

The rough-shaping for the ray surface is complete. I now hog out waste below the hub and bottom rays, making the transition to the rail on the carcase. A ⅜-in. bench chisel works well for bringing this surface down to the line scribed earlier in the layout (see photo 6 on p. 121).

With the scallops and hub incised and the ray surface formed, I start carving the individual rays. A ray, in cross section, has a crowned shape. The height of the crown remains constant as the ray broadens, expanding from the hub to the scalloped edge. I begin carving the rays by defining the lines with a V parting tool (see photo 7 on p. 121). Because of the serpentine sur-

There are three carved fans on this highboy: one on the center drawer of the upper case, one on the center drawer of the base, and a third, much smaller, one at the top of the scroll board (see the drawing on p. 124).

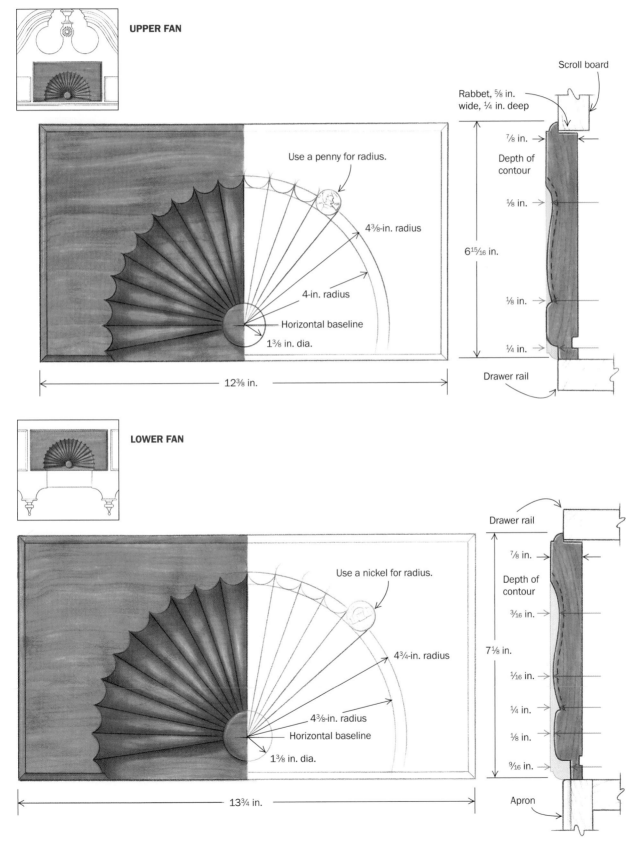

UPPER FAN

Use a penny for radius.

4³⁄₈-in. radius

4-in. radius

Horizontal baseline

1³⁄₈ in. dia.

12³⁄₈ in.

Scroll board

Rabbet, ⁵⁄₈ in. wide, ¼ in. deep

⁷⁄₈ in.

Depth of contour

¹⁄₈ in.

6¹⁵⁄₁₆ in.

¹⁄₈ in.

¼ in.

Drawer rail

LOWER FAN

Use a nickel for radius.

4³⁄₄-in. radius

4³⁄₈-in. radius

Horizontal baseline

1³⁄₈ in. dia.

13³⁄₄ in.

Drawer rail

⁷⁄₈ in.

Depth of contour

³⁄₁₆ in.

7¹⁄₈ in.

¹⁄₁₆ in.

¼ in.

¹⁄₈ in.

⁹⁄₁₆ in.

Apron

face, I have to change the tool direction so that I am always cutting downhill in relation to the grain. This helps me avoid lifting a big chip or having the wood split far ahead of the tool.

I use gouges to shape the rays. Starting from the V on either side, I cut along the ray, gradually working it to a rough convex shape (see photo 8 on the facing page). The faceted surface is smoothed into a continuous curve.

The hub is slightly tapered and crowned, but this detail is carved last. The hub can get nicked if you get too close with a V parting tool or a gouge. These nicks are cut away with the final shaping. Periodically,

■ Carving the Fans

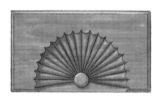

Fans carved into drawer fronts at the top and bottom of the case help give the highboy its distinctive look. The 20 rays in each fan are laid out and carved on a serpentine background.

1. A coin for the scalloped edge—A penny is the right size for the upper drawer fan. A nickel fits the lower fan.

2. A scribe line marks the depth of the carved surface below the fan. This area forms the transition between the fan and the case rail.

3. To prevent wood from splintering into the hub surface, outline this area with carving tools.

4. Shape the fan background across the grain. Developing the S-shaped surface with mostly cross-grain cutting gives greater control over the tool.

5. Smooth the surface with a sculptor's rasp. A uniform surface makes carving the fan's rays easier.

I check the rays to make them the same, deepening the V between rays where it's needed. I crown the surface of the hub and taper the sides slightly. Finally, rifflers and sandpaper complete the fan (see photo 9 below).

FLAME FINIALS
START ON THE LATHE

These finials use the burning-torch motif that's seen on many high chests and tall clocks. The lower part of the finial is an urn, and the twist above it represents a

6. Use a bench chisel to remove the waste below the fan. This surface provides the transition from the carved drawer to the case rail.

7. A V parting tool is used to define the rays. Because the surface is S-shaped, wood grain can change direction. Take care not to run tools against the grain, which could cause tearout.

8. A successful fan carving is symmetrical. Shape the rays so they appear uniform in width and depth.

9. Sand the fan. The scallops and hub should not be rounded over.

flame. The overall shape is developed on the lathe, and the flame is then carved at the bench. The finials are made of 2¾-in.-sq. cherry stock.

I start by cutting the billets about 2 in. longer than the overall length of the completed finial (see the bottom drawing on the facing page), and then locating the center points for mounting them on the lathe. I turn the finial to shape and use a parting tool to establish the key diameters and gouges to cut and blend the sections together.

I turn a ½-in.-dia. by 1-in.-long tenon on the end of the urn, nearest the headstock. Then I turn the tip of the flame to ¼ in. dia. and sand the entire finial. Even though the flame surface will be carved, a smooth surface makes it easier to lay out the twist.

The flame detail is somewhat like a screw thread—four grooves spiral up from the urn to converge at the tip to a point. Each groove (or flute) makes one complete turn. To lay out the flame, I mark the middle of the length of the turning. Then, using the indexing head on my lathe to hold the stock in position, I make four longitudinal lines at 90° intervals. Using these lines on the flame section, I create the helical flutes by wrapping a strip of paper around the flame portion and scribing a line along the edge of the paper (see photo 1 on the facing page). After all four helical lines are drawn, I blend the starting and ending points by eye. Now I can remove the turning from the lathe and saw off the waste at the ends.

CARVE THE FLAME WITH GOUGES

Holding turned pieces for carving can be a problem. The best solution I've found is to drill a hole slightly smaller than the finial tenon in a piece of scrap the size of a short 2x4 and jam the finial's round tenon into it.

I can now clamp the scrap stock in my vise to position the finial at a comfortable angle and height.

I start defining the helix with a narrow gouge (see photo 2 on the facing page), and then I work up to a gouge that is slightly smaller than the flute width (see photo 3 on the facing page). Be careful not to cut into the helical layout line because this will alter the profile of the flame. I work each flute one at a time to avoid any mix-ups. After the flutes are carved, I smooth them with a round rasp and sandpaper.

MAKE THE WAIST MOLDING

When the fans and finials are completed, it's time to return to the highboy and finish the remaining details: the waist molding, plinths, and finial caps.

The waist molding visually eases the transition between the base and the upper case. The molding, on the front and both sides of the case, also has a practical purpose. It keys the upper case to the base. I make the bead-and-cove profile on a shaper (see the waist-molding drawing detail on p. 124). About 7 ft. of stock is needed to frame the front and sides.

To install the molding, I center the upper case on the base with the backs flush. This leaves a 1-in. gap on the front and sides to cover with the waist molding. I now measure and cut the molding stock. The molding is glued and nailed (with 4d cut nails) to the base unit. When the molding is in place, it's not necessary to fasten the upper case to the base.

MAKE THE PLINTHS, AND MOUNT THE FINIALS

The finials on the upper corners of the bonnet sit atop small pedestals, also called plinths. Each plinth is a 1½-in.-sq. by 1-in.-tall cherry block with a ½-in.-dia. hole bored through the top center for the finial

1. A strip of paper wrapped around the finial creates a helix. The ends of the helices are brought to a point by eye.

2. Begin carving with a narrow veiner. Be careful not to cut into layout lines.

3. To form the flute, remove waste from between the helical grooves with a larger gouge.

FINIAL LAYOUT

Three flame finials cap the top of the upper case. Each has four flutes, which make one complete turn around the finial.

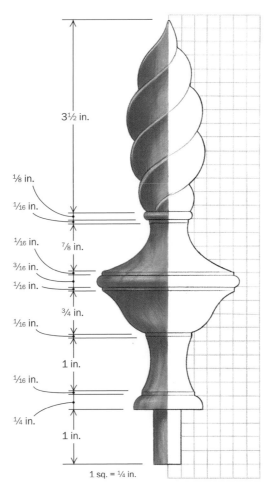

3½ in.

⅛ in.

1/16 in.

1/16 in.   ⅞ in.

3/16 in.

1/16 in.

3/4 in.

1/16 in.

1 in.

1/16 in.

1/4 in.

1 in.

1 sq. = ¼ in.

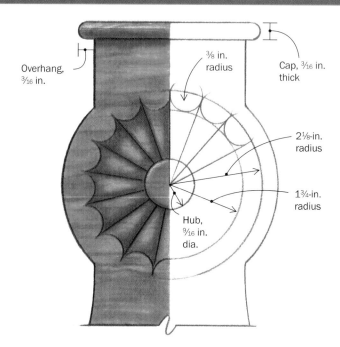

SCROLL-BOARD FAN

A carved fan punctuates the top of the scroll board. The fan has an outside radius of 2⅛ in. and a total of 17 rays.

Overhang, ³⁄₁₆ in.

³⁄₈ in. radius

Cap, ³⁄₁₆ in. thick

2⅛-in. radius

1¾-in. radius

Hub, ⁹⁄₁₆ in. dia.

PLINTH AND FINIAL CAP

The plinth and the finial cap provide a base for the finial.

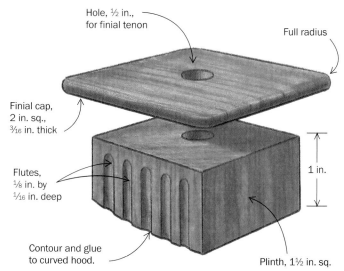

Hole, ½ in., for finial tenon

Full radius

Finial cap, 2 in. sq., ³⁄₁₆ in. thick

Flutes, ⅛ in. by ¹⁄₁₆ in. deep

1 in.

Contour and glue to curved hood.

Plinth, 1½ in. sq.

WAIST MOLDING

This molding holds the upper case in place on the base unit. It also provides the visual transition between these two large masses.

1 sq. = ¼ in.

DROP FINIAL

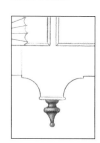

Tenons, ½ in. dia., attach two drop finials to the apron of the highboy's base. The finials are set on cap pieces ³⁄₁₆ in. thick.

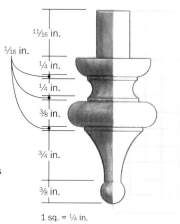

11⁄₁₆ in.

¹⁄₁₆ in.

¼ in.

¼ in.

⅜ in.

¾ in.

⅜ in.

1 sq. = ¼ in.

tenon. Five ⅛-in.-wide, evenly spaced flutes are carved into the front face (see the plinth and finial cap drawing on the facing page).

The only trick to making the plinths is scribing the bottom of the plinth block to the curved hood, making certain that the plinth sits plumb. Here's what I do: Because the plinth is rather stubby, I temporarily fit a 2-ft.-long dowel into the hole in the plinth block. I use this long dowel as a sighting device.

I position the plinth block in the corner of the bonnet and, holding the dowel plumb, scribe the block to the bonnet curve. Because there's not much stock to remove to the scribe line, I use my belt sander. Then I glue the plinth blocks to the bonnet hood with contact cement—yellow glue doesn't work as well for this end-grain joint.

All five finials (three upper and two drop finials on the base) sit directly on a plinth cap. Each cap is a small piece of cherry stock, 3/16 in. thick with a full radius on all edges. The caps overhang the bases on which they are mounted by 3/16 in. on each side. A ½-in. hole is bored in the center for the finial tenon, and the caps are glued and nailed with brads to the plinths.

I don't glue the finials in place, so they can be removed when the highboy is moved. They are less likely to break or be damaged that way. Placing the finials on the highboy completes the woodworking portion of this project.

APPLY THE FINISH

Finish is such a personal preference. Advocates speak passionately for their favorite finishing materials and techniques. For me, the choice is simple—I use shellac. It's hard to beat for depth, luster, and authenticity. Before applying the finish, I wet the surfaces to raise the grain. After the surfaces dry, I sand away the fuzz. I then apply a water-based aniline dye.

If you're unfamiliar with aniline dyes, experiment on scrap first to check the color. These dyes produce beautifully clear and vibrant colors, but they won't behave exactly like the oil-based pigmented stains you may be used to. It's easy to get lap marks if you're not careful. Using several coats of diluted dye is more predictable than trying to get the right color in a single coat.

After the dye is dry, I lightly rub the surface with a Scotch-Brite™ pad to remove any additional raised grain. I then apply an oil-based glazing stain. Unlike the dye, glazing stain is very forgiving. It evens the base color and gives the look of 100 years of patina. I leave some residue in cracks and crevices to add to the aging effect.

After a 24-hour drying period, I start padding on shellac with a soft cloth. Between each coat of shellac, I lightly sand with a fine Scotch-Brite pad and wipe the surface with a clean cloth. I used four coats of shellac on this highboy. Customers often request a final waxed surface. It certainly imparts a satiny depth, but wax attracts dust and fingerprints and always needs periodic rewaxing. I usually skip it.

Inspiration

Your work is a creative outlet. Sometimes you want to make a quick, simple project, sometimes you want to challenge yourself with an elaborate piece, and sometimes you're just not sure what you're looking for. That's where this section comes in. You'll find a variety of examples here to inspire you, and the specifications and design information will help you make the leap from inspiration to reality.

DOUG MOOBERRY AND KEVIN ARNOLD

Salem Secretary in Figured Mahogany

We have wanted to make a great desk and bookcase ever since we started making furniture together in the early 1980s. We needed just three things: someone to pay us, a great desk and bookcase to copy, and wood to blow everybody away.

The first part, finding the collector—well, everyone knows what that's about, but finally a longtime customer became interested. The second part—which desk to copy—was up to our client. We looked at different examples of cases from Newport and Philadelphia, but the double oxbow fronts of Salem and Boston were just too seductive to pass up.

We found a wonderful color photograph with dimensions in American Furniture in the Kaufman Collection, which showed the desk open and closed. This photograph and others in Israel Sacks' American Antiques books were enough for us to create our variation on these masterpieces.

The last element was what wood to use; as it turned out, we had some nice pieces of mahogany tucked away in the barn for just the right project. For the upper doors, we bookmatched solid crotch mahogany panels.

The double oxbow drawer fronts were sawn from 2¼-in.-thick crotch mahogany—consecutive boards, naturally. For the remainder of the case we used two 30-in.-wide mahogany boards 18 ft. long, sawn consecutively out of the log and therefore consistent in color and grain. Local poplar is the secondary wood.

We have restored many desks, and the knowledge we gained doing that helped fill in where the photographs and dimensions left off. We drew the desk full size, mainly to make sure its 98-in. height would fit into the client's house. We found that it would, and building started. The hardware and locks were custom-made in England and took forever to arrive. When they finally

SPECIFICATIONS

- **DIMENSIONS**
  46 in. wide, 26 in. deep, and 98 in. high.

- **MATERIALS**
  Mahogany, poplar, and brass.

- **FINISH**
  Aniline dye, shellac, and paste wax.

A FLOCK OF PIGEONHOLES. One advantage of a secretary this size is beautifully appointed storage space, including 13 secret compartments.

appeared, we refiled the brasses and repolished them to get the patina we wanted.

As construction began, we invited our client to visit the shop from time to time and see our progress. To him, watching the piece unfold was an important part of becoming the desk's owner. Every so often, on sunny days, he would ride out to our shop on his motorcycle to see how things were progressing.

Inside are 13 secret drawers. When we delivered the desk, we filled the secret drawer that was hardest to find with Godiva™ chocolate gold coins and waited for them to be discovered.

THE CUSTOM-MADE BRASSES FROM ENGLAND had to be bent to conform to the double oxbow drawer fronts.

WOOD ON FIRE. The flaming crotch mahogany adds visual punch to the facade of this spectacular secretary, based on one built in Salem, Mass.

WALTER RAYNES AND CARL CLINTON

18th-Century Card Table

MIRROR IMAGES. A bit anachronistic, card tables today are often placed against a wall while they're half open, like a demilune, to display the intricate inlay work on the tabletop.

SPECIFICATIONS

■ DIMENSIONS
36 in. in diameter (open) and 28 in. high.

■ MATERIALS
Mahogany and mahogany veneer, poplar, and the following veneers used for the inlays: walnut, holly, rosewood, curly maple, and ebony.

■ FINISH
French polish.

Work is where you find it. A customer of ours spotted a Federal-style card table in our storeroom while waiting for a repair job that should have been finished. The customer loved the table and commissioned us to build a similar one on the spot.

Card tables often had highly decorated tops that were visible when folded in half and placed against the wall. The interiors usually were utilitarian and sometimes were covered with baize (a feltlike fabric woven out of wool or cotton) to provide a better surface for playing cards.

This table is a marriage of New York and Baltimore styles of the late 18th century

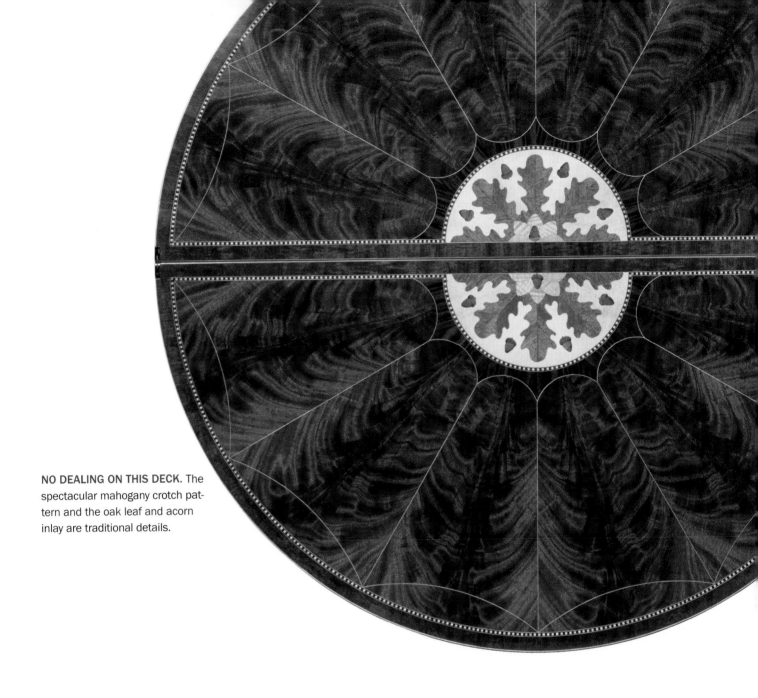

NO DEALING ON THIS DECK. The spectacular mahogany crotch pattern and the oak leaf and acorn inlay are traditional details.

(about 1790 to 1800). The bell-flower inlays on the legs are more of a Baltimore style, while the circular top with pie-shaped wedges of crotch mahogany, the central field of oak and acorn inlays, and the dentil stringing is more associated with tables built in New York.

Never slaves to tradition, however, we made some changes. The interior of the table (the flat part when open) is the most spectacular, made to be seen and not for playing cards. (The owner uses it to display a collection of decorative glass.) We also made the legs more slender than the originals to give the table a lighter look, and we reduced the overhang of the top to show off the inlay work in the apron.

In another departure from tradition, we reversed the grain direction of the crotch mahogany veneer. Purists may cringe when they see this (it certainly distressed another client of ours—an antiques dealer), but we think these changes, plus the more than 200 hours of work that went into this piece, resulted in a spectacular table.

Inspiration

JEFFREY P. GREENE

A Desk with Distinguished Ancestry

A good desk was essential to any businessman in the 18th century, and the level of its elegance was a measure of status and success. This was especially true in bustling Newport, R.I., at the time New England's second largest city after Boston.

Newport in the 18th century was a hive of activity. Its streets and wharves were crowded with commerce, and two Quaker families—the Goddards and the Townsends—built much of the best furniture for the rising merchant class. It is little wonder, therefore, that these two preeminent cabinet-making families were hired to build many slant-front desks like this one.

The desk is a faithful replica of one built between 1760 and 1790 and authenticated to John Townsend. (The original is at the John Brown house in Providence.) Although the Goddards and the Townsends are best known for their mahogany furniture, they did use other woods, such as soft maple. The maple boards I used for this

SPECIFICATIONS

■ DIMENSIONS
38½ in. long, 21¼ in. wide, and 41½ in. high.

■ MATERIALS
Soft tiger maple, eastern white pine, and brass.

■ FINISH
Aniline dye and shellac.

A "BLOCKED" INTERIOR. In a signature of the Goddard and Townsend style, the inside drawers are "blocked," which means the carved shells and panels are alternately raised and recessed.

THE LAPTOP OF THE 18TH CENTURY. A slant-front desk, like this one designed by John Townsend of Newport, was a requirement for merchants and businessmen of the time.

replication were sawn from one tree and kept in sequence for consistent figure.

The design genius of the Goddards and the Townsends resided in their ability to infuse a simple form with the utmost refinement. The exterior of the desk has carefully graduated drawers, a simple but pronounced base molding and ogee feet of exceptional form and grace. The outside is void of ornament, with the exception of the bold brass pull plates and escutcheons.

The interior is characteristically powerful but orderly. The blocking, the alternately raised and recessed panels, adds interest to what would otherwise be a plain array of drawers and pigeonholes. The blocking is smoothly integrated from the writing surface up to the three carved shells. The scrolled fronts of the pigeonhole dividers add to the three-dimensional effect of the interior and connect the lower drawers to the valances with flair.

While building this desk, I was fortunate to have a maple chest of drawers attributed to John Townsend in my workshop. The similarities between the two pieces, and the privilege of having an original close at hand, proved inspirational.

A MULTITUDE OF DRAWERS. There are 17 drawers on the inside of this desk (including three behind the carved door), plus a sliding panel, or well, for access to the top drawer while the lid is open.

ROB WIGGENHORN

Chippendale Dining Chairs

W e had always wanted a set of Chippendale dining chairs, but those store prices…WOW! As virtually my first serious furniture-making project, a set of four dining chairs seemed like a bit of a challenge. But after studying an article on making Chippendale chairs, I was confident I could do it. The project took me many months. But more than any project I've tackled since, these chairs provided a genuine education, specifically in the use of hand tools. And in retrospect, this was an excellent first project.

Before starting, I looked through countless books on chairs to find the right design. There was no single chair that had all of the features I was looking for: a pierced Gothic back, a carved scroll crest rail, a serpentine front seat rail, and Marlborough legs. Marlborough legs were either straight, square legs, or square-tapered legs, and they usually terminated in a block or plinth. Chippendale occasionally would use Marlborough legs instead of cabriole legs. After combining these elements into a design I liked, I created full-scale drawings and templates using art board and heavy Mylar™. The templates let me trace each part with assured repeatability.

The steam-bending of the back splat, done with a unique setup of furnace pipe, camp stove, and PVC plumbing, actually was quite fun. (For more on the steam box, see the sidebar on p. 141.) However, the

SCULPTING THE CREST RAIL INTO THE BACK POSTS required lots of work with a rasp after the chair had been glued up. Although nerve-racking, the author found this work to be the most rewarding aspect of building the chair.

SPECIFICATIONS

- **DIMENSIONS**
  20 in. wide, 18 in. deep, and 39½ in. high.

- **MATERIALS**
  Walnut and woven cotton upholstery.

- **FINISH**
  Sam Maloof's oil/wax.

CHIPPENDALE DINING CHAIR. By combining elements from a variety of different Chippendale-era chairs, the maker was able to create a style that he found pleasing and true to the era.

THE SERPENTINE FRONT SEAT RAIL is mortised and tenoned to the Marlborough leg. The straight, square shape of the Marlborough leg often was used in place of a cabriole leg on Chippendale furniture.

task that proved to be the most interesting was the hand-shaping of the crest rail and the leg posts. There is something quite unsettling about taking a wood rasp to the back of a chair and aggressively removing material. Much of this work cannot be done until everything is glued up, when there is no turning back. The creative sculpting, smoothing, and blending of the crest-rail contours into the back posts was a very rewarding feeling, like no other project I have completed since.

The upholstery work was straightforward. Seat frames of eastern maple were fit into rabbets in the chair, leaving about ⅛-in. clearance all around for the upholstery. In spite of my best efforts to make all chairs identical, I had to custom-fit each seat frame.

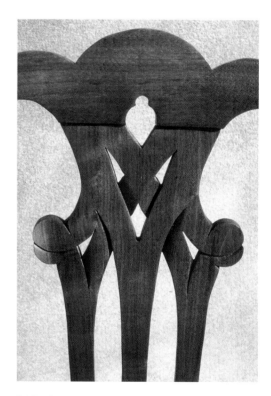

BACK SPLATS ARE STEAM-BENT. The maker carved details into the back splats after splats were bent to shape in a simple steam box.

■ A SIMPLE STEAM BOX

I decided to steam-bend the back splats of my Chippendale chairs, rather than make the splats from glued-up laminations, because I didn't want layers of wood to show in the relief carving. The splats were made from ½-in.-thick walnut. I cut out the profile before putting the splats in my shop-made steam box, but I didn't do any carving until later.

The steam box was easy to make. The box itself is a section of sheet-metal stovepipe that I forced into a rectangular shape with the help of 2x4 plugs at each end (see the drawing at right). I also needed a good, gas camp stove, two new 1-gal. paint cans, one with a lid, and about 6 ft. of ¾-in.-dia. PVC pipe. The lid has a hole in the top for the PVC pipe and goes on the paint can over the camp stove. The pipe should fit snugly.

Inside the box, the chair splat rested on two ½-in. thick blocks so that steam could flow freely around the wood. The steam-inlet end of the box was propped up slightly to allow water condensing inside the box to drain down to the other end. Duct tape keeps the box from leaking steam, and I added water periodically to the can over the camp stove.

After two hours of steaming, I removed the splat and clamped it immediately in a form made from 2x6s. The radius on the form was

tighter than what I wanted on the finished splat to allow for a little spring-back after the wood came out of the form. The deflection on each finished splat needed to be ½ in., so I cut out the 2x6s for the form with a deflection of

⅞ in. When the wood sprang back, it was just right. After overnight clamping in the form, the splats were ready for carving. I could do one splat at a time, so the bending for all four chairs took four evenings.

■ Steam Box from Stovepipe

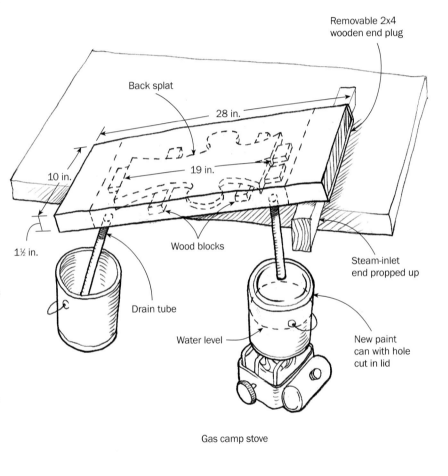

Removable 2x4 wooden end plug

Back splat

28 in.

19 in.

10 in.

1½ in.

Wood blocks

Drain tube

Water level

Steam-inlet end propped up

New paint can with hole cut in lid

Gas camp stove

PAUL ZENATY

Curly Maple Secretary

RICHLY FIGURED WOOD AND SKILLFUL execution create a harmonious whole.

Being of Czech descent, I've long been exposed to the elegant, formal lines of central European furniture. My familiarity and appreciation for these classical forms led me to become a cabinet- and furniture maker and instilled in me a love of both European and early American antiques.

The inspiration for this piece came while viewing an exhibit of 18th-century Portsmouth, N.H., furniture. The fine lines of a breakfront with Sheraton window bars and a little knee-hole desk sparked my imagination and convinced me to set to work on this secretary.

I chose curly maple and used a flat-top design as opposed to a bonnet top because I live in an 1870s farmhouse with 7-ft. ceil-

SPECIFICATIONS

■ DIMENSIONS
45⅞ in. wide, 20⅝ in. deep, and
81⅛ in. high.

■ MATERIALS
Curly maple, with secondary woods of
pine and poplar.

■ FINISH
Minwax™ colonial maple and red
mahogany stains; nitrocellulose lacquer,
and lemon oil.

SIMPLE YET REFINED. The maker's secretary in curly maple is a traditionally inspired case piece. Elements from several 18th-century Portsmouth, N. H., antiques found their way to his creation.

ings. I used shiplapped boards for the backs of both the top and bottom pieces of the secretary because shiplapping is in keeping with the spirit and era of the secretary and because the back is visible through the glass doors of the upper case.

The upper case is attached to the desk with solid brass straps mortised into the backs of both pieces. I breadboarded the ends of the desk lid to keep it flat while still allowing for cross-grain movement. The drawers in the desk's work area sweep back twice from the vertical drawers on the outside. The two Doric columns that frame the fan-carved door at center are the fronts for secret drawers, which are released with touch catches.

The five lower drawers all feature hand-cut dovetails (as do the small drawers behind the desk lid) and have cocked beads around them. The drawer runners are attached to the carcase sides with sliding dovetails and are mortised into the drawer dividers, which are dovetailed to the carcase.

■ Curly Maple Secretary

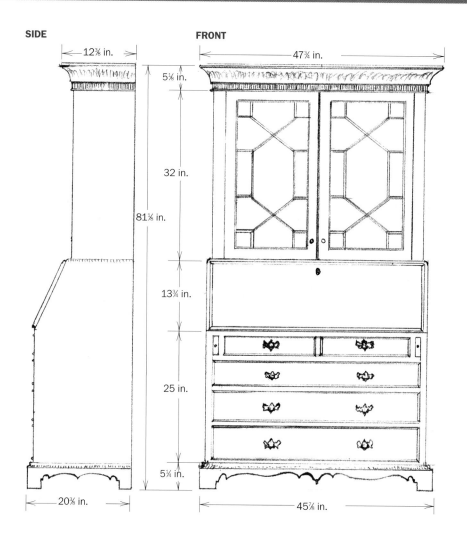

CHRIS ARATO AND ROBERT McCULLOUGH

Philadelphia Highboy

When the two of us worked at Irion Company Furnituremakers in Pennsylvania, we collaborated on a lot of furniture. Then Chris moved to far northern Maine, and Rob opened his own carving shop. Collaboration over? Not yet. We both still do plenty of work for Irion Company, and last year when the company wanted a showpiece Philadelphia Chippendale highboy, we were asked to build it. No problem. Chris would do the cabinetmaking on the Canadian border,

SPECIFICATIONS

■ DIMENSIONS
44¼ in. wide, 23 in. deep and 95½ in. high.

■ MATERIALS
Mahogany and crotch mahogany with poplar secondary wood.

■ FINISH
Aniline dye, pigmented stain, and shellac.

CUTTING EDGE AT THE TIME OF THE REVOLUTION. Two 18th-century Philadelphia Chippendale highboys were the basis for this 20th-century reproduction. The makers studied the originals in photographs and blended details and dimensions to arrive at their design.

ALWAYS FACE YOUR AUDIENCE. McCullough carved this lower drawer front, which is below eye level, with a slight upward tilt. He did the opposite for the carving on the upper drawer.

WELL-TRAVELED LEGS. The highboy was a collaboration between two woodworkers who live 800 miles apart. The cabriole legs were roughed out in Maine, mailed to Pennsylvania for carving and sent back to Maine to be attached to the case.

and Rob would do the carving 800 miles to the south.

The collaboration began on the telephone, as we zeroed in on which highboy we'd like to build. We chose two very similar Philadelphia highboys, one in a collection in the East, the other in the Midwest. Instead of copying either one, we blended the two. We each had photos of the originals and began by scaling the photos and comparing the dimensions we came up with. When we had them nailed down, we drew various details on tracing paper and sent them back and forth. When one of us received a sketch of a leg, midmolding, or gooseneck in the mail, he'd lay it over his own sketch to see how closely we were thinking. In most cases, very closely.

When the piece got underway, the packages traveling through the mail got heavier. Chris roughed out the cabriole legs and cut the joints for them. Then he popped the legs in the mail so that Rob could carve them. The carved drawer fronts were also

AT THE PINNACLE OF THE CARVER'S ART. As with other carving, the trick with a cartouche, the ornament at the top of the highboy, is to make the composition strong enough to attract the eye from across the room, and the detail clean enough to satisfy scrutiny from a few feet away.

well-traveled. Chris milled blanks for them and sent them south. Rob did the flower, leaf and tendril carving and sent them back north. Chris cut the dovetails and assembled the drawers.

The cartouche and the flame finials are very fragile, so we didn't mail them. We waited until Chris drove the completed highboy down to Pennsylvania, where Kendl Monn of Irion Company applied the finish. Then, like the trimming on a Christmas tree, the finials and the cartouche took their places on top of the piece.

G. R. CLIDENCE

Sheraton Field Bed

Since the late 1700s, when Thomas Sheraton popularized the style, the field bed has always surpassed the basic requirement of providing a good night's rest. It was designed for field generals and aristocratic types with discriminating sleeping habits. In response to the demands of their wealthy clients, furniture makers of the period tried to outdo each other by adding decorative details. As a result, few of these beds were the same, so I had lots of latitude in designing one.

The biggest challenge was to marry today's practical sleeping requirements with the appearance of a genuine period piece. Bed sizes in the 18th century were smaller and not standardized as they are today. Today's sleepers also prefer higher headboards than did our forebears. These factors made it necessary to enlarge and reproportion the posts to appear correct in relation to the rest of the bed.

The posts shown here were made from one large mahogany plank. Each post was turned and reeded in two sections and then joined back together. The decoration on the posts is moderate for the period. In early versions of the field bed, only the posts at the foot of the bed were turned and sometimes reeded. Later, as the design accumulated layers of adornment, all four posts were reeded or fluted, and some had elaborate foliage carvings.

Original beds also used a rope mesh to hold the mattress. The ropes were tightly tensioned, so the sides had to be thick, sometimes 3 in. or 4 in. square. I preserved this feature, even though it was unnecessary because the mattress sits on a platform, not on a rope mesh.

Mattresses today are thicker than 18th-century mattresses, so the platform between the bed rails had to be recessed to preserve the original look. I beveled the inside edge

SPECIFICATIONS

■ DIMENSIONS
87 in. long, 67 in. wide, and 82 in. high.

■ MATERIALS
Mahogany, oak, and brass.

■ FINISH
Stain and flat polyurethane rubbed with gel varnish.

A BED WORTHY OF A GENERAL. The inspiration for this canopy bed was the "field bed" designed in the late 1700s by Thomas Sheraton and used by generals in the military.

of the rails to make it easier to tuck in the sheets and the blankets.

The canopy framework was another challenge. In originals I had seen, the serpentine canopy is sawn and hinged in the middle for mobility and ease of construction. To me, these looked bulky and crude, although they were usually hidden behind the canopy dressing. Instead, I steam-bent the oak canopy to the serpentine shape, and I chamfered the edges. This canopy frame is sturdy but a little more graceful than some of the originals. It is beautiful either left uncovered or partially visible through lace hangings.

UPDATING A CLASSIC. Modern beds are bigger than those of the early 1800s, which meant the author had to redesign the posts and the headboard to preserve the original proportions.

BED RAILS ARE STURDY. In original beds of the Sheraton period, the rails were made out of thick stock to support a taught rope mesh, which held the mattress. In this bed, the mattress sits on a platform, but the heavy rails were preserved for historical accuracy.

ADORNMENTS ARE IN THE BEDPOSTS.
Sheraton-style field beds had varying amounts of decoration, depending on the builder. Here the posts are turned and reeded and topped by a finial.

LANCE PATTERSON

Mahogany Federal Sideboard

The man who asked me to make this sideboard dictated size, shape, style, and type of wood. Proportion, decoration, and construction were left to me.

The sideboard was to be a small, D-shaped Federal piece made of mahogany. I checked my memory and the library for pictures of such sideboards. I feel more comfortable when I find some precedent for my design choices. But I do not like to make close copies. To me, it's missing the point of this furniture to make exact copies because fur-niture makers who built the original Federal pieces made them different to suit individual customers.

I borrowed the D-shaped top and the form of the front with the fans on spandrel brackets from Thomas Sheraton, but I sim-plified it by having only two cupboards flanking one central drawer and by including simpler, straight-tapered Hepplewhite legs.

I used dark mahogany swirl veneers on the cupboard doors and the drawer front, and bright, large, deeply shaded holly span-

SHERATON MEETS HEPPLEWHITE. The D-shaped top and the fan decoration in this Federal sideboard were inspired by Thomas Sheraton; the leg design was borrowed from George Hepplewhite.

drel fans to catch the eye and invite people in for a closer look.

I like my designs to be strong visually. All of the lines of this sideboard are accented with inlaid stringing or bandings, and all of the corners on the front are further accented with fan inlays. The long-petaled bellflowers on the legs are similar to period ones on some pieces from Baltimore or Annapolis, Maryland. I particularly liked the distinctive sand shading of the top tip of the long central petal and the bottom tips of the side petals. However, I did try to restrain the number of design elements and colors.

I chose the simplest Hepplewhite drawer pulls, and the escutcheons are inlaid ivory, which was recycled from old piano-key covers. (When recycled ivory is not available, I use bleached cow bone.) The decoration ties the piece together by accenting all visible surfaces with related lines and colors, but clearly the front is designed for primary visual interest.

A FEDERAL CASE. The holly inlay, the shaded fans, and the long-petaled bellflowers unify the sideboard by accenting visible surfaces with related lines and colors.

COOPERED DOORS REQUIRE A GOOD JIG

There are two secrets to making the coopered doors on my mahogany federal sideboard: a core of quarter-sawn wood with consistent grain direction for easy planing, and a good jig for the glue-up.

The simple clamping jig uses a filler piece on one end and opposing wedges on the other end to press the staves of the coopered panel together. The jig consists of ¾-in. plywood clamping stations fixed to a base of flat plywood (or MDF) at 8-in. to 12-in. intervals.

I bandsaw clamping stations in a stack to create identical forms for the outside curvature of the staves. The clamping stations must be parallel to each other, so I lay out their positions on the base and screw them onto the base from underneath.

The curvature of the jig depends on the final shape of the doors and the width of the staves. If you want to be precise, check out your setup by making a full-sized drawing that includes the actual stave width. To further ensure a tight fit in the cabinet, however, I find that it is much better—and easier—to trim the rails and top and bottom of the case to the door, rather than trim the door to fit.

The size of the door on this sideboard required only two clamping stations. Larger doors with longer staves might demand more stations. Also, as shown in the photo, I doubled up the plywood for each station, but that was overdoing it.

The door started with an 8/4 poplar board, which I jointed and surfaced to 1¾ inches. I ripped it into ⅞-inch staves, which are folded out in book fashion. The edges are then ripped to the approximate coopering angle and hand planed to fit the form. The edge joints are all glued at the same time and are clamped with the aid of wedges at one end of the form.

After the glue sets, the outside of the core is planed with the grain and spokeshaved across the grain. The inside of the core is shaped and smoothed with a round-bottomed scrub plane and spokeshave.

THE COOPER'S ART. Coopering is taken from the craft of making wooden casks and tubs. Coopered doors for the sideboard (above) were made in a simple, two-station form (below).

E. JEFF JUSTIS, JR.

Queen Anne Hall Table

A narrow hallway in our home needed a table to hold family pictures and a guest book, prompting the design of this Queen Anne style piece.

I wanted to keep the width of the table to 15 in. or less so there would be enough room for people to pass by easily. Length was not critical, and in my initial drawings I settled on 41 in., which to me created the most pleasing proportions. I made the legs delicate but broadened the footprint as much as possible for stability.

The apron is made out of two pieces that are glued together. I made the lower portion out of thicker stock. After band-sawing the scrolled shape, I glued it to the upper apron. I also beveled the lower, inside edge of the apron to make it look less bulky. The tenons are pinned with traditional square pegs.

I made the top out of a 16-in.-wide plank of mahogany and rounded the corners with a 2-in. radius to protect passersby. The edge is molded for a lighter look; I didn't want this tall, narrow piece to seem top-heavy.

LEGS ARE SLENDER BUT STRONG. The padded feet on these delicate Queen Anne-style legs were left as large as possible to give the narrow table added stability.

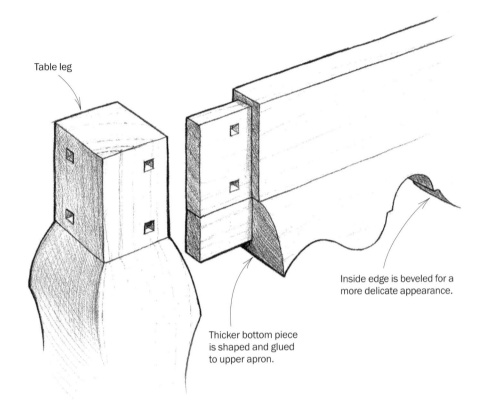

Table leg

Thicker bottom piece
is shaped and glued
to upper apron.

Inside edge is beveled for a
more delicate appearance.

**A WIDE TABLE WOULDN'T
FIT.** Designed for a narrow hallway, this table had to be 15 in.
wide or less.

SPECIFICATIONS

■ DIMENSIONS
41 in. long, $14^{13}\!/_{16}$ in. wide, and
32 in. high.

■ MATERIALS
Mahogany.

■ FINISH
Watco Oil and red mahogany filler.

PETER VAN BECKUM

Sheraton Armchair

The original of this Sheraton armchair was made by Samuel McIntire within a year or two of 1800. McIntire (1757–1811), who ran a shop in Salem, Mass., designed and built houses as well as furniture, and the two pursuits cross-pollinated. The carved basket of fruit against a punched background on the crest rail of the chair is a motif also found on mantels he designed.

My copy is made from two boards of Honduras mahogany. All the visible parts, except the backsplat, came from a straight-grained 8/4 plank. I chose an unexciting wood because the design has such dynamic shapes and negative spaces. I wanted to accentuate them rather than show off dramatic wood grain. Also, the straight-grained wood provided strength in a chair whose fine dimensions place it just above the threshold of structural requirements.

I cut and carved the splat, with its pattern of intersecting Gothic arches, from a single piece of 4/4 mahogany. I could have carved it from glued up boards, but I wanted to avoid joint lines for appearance's sake. Using a single board also makes the carving a little easier. Once you've figured out what the grain is doing and adjusted your carving

DESIGNING WITH A BUILDER'S EYE. The architectural quality of the backsplat in this copy of a Samuel McIntire armchair is no accident. McIntire designed buildings as well as furniture.

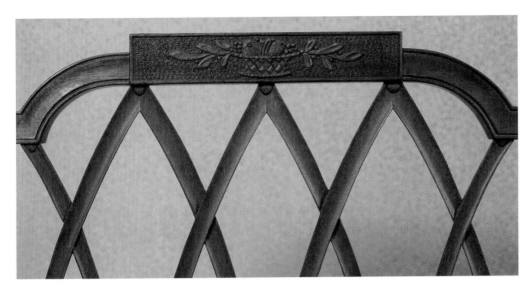

CARVING A PLACE IN HISTORY. Samuel McIntire's masterful shaping and carving (reproduced here by the author) made him famous in and around Salem, Mass., at the end of the 18th century.

technique, you're set, because the grain will be fairly similar throughout.

The fabric of the seat is haircloth, a combination of cotton and horsehair. The stuffing is curled horsehair. Both are authentic to the period. Ash rails and corner blocks are hidden beneath the upholstery. Ash holds tacks well and tolerates repeated upholstering.

The chair's simple, straight-tapered legs provide a nice visual base and don't require that a lot of labor be lavished on a part of the chair that is often out of sight. They leave the greatest embellishment for the splat, a dining chair's most prominent element.

ALL THE CURVES ARE ABOVE THE SEAT. McIntire used straight lines in the legs and stretchers to make the curving back and arms more expressive by contrast.

SPECIFICATIONS

- **DIMENSIONS**
  23 in. wide, 20½ in. deep, and 38 in. high.

- **MATERIALS**
  Honduras mahogany, ash, cotton, and horsehair-blend fabric, curled horsehair stuffing, and brass tacks.

- **FINISH**
  Boiled linseed oil.

WILLIAM E. LOCKE

Townsend Kneehole Desk

ECONOMY OF MAHOGANY.
By cutting carefully, the author squeezed all the primary wood for this desk from a single board 12 ft. long, 3 in. thick, and 26 in. wide.

SPECIFICATIONS

■ DIMENSIONS
36½ in. wide, 20½ in. deep, and 33½ in. high.

■ MATERIALS
Mahogany and maple.

■ FINISH
Shellac.

To call this piece of furniture a desk is misleading. The original was never intended to be used as a desk at all. Most likely, it served as a chest of drawers or a bureau table. Of the 50 or so original examples of the form known to exist, only four have a pull-out, drop-front desk section in the top drawer. Nevertheless, the term kneehole desk or just kneehole is commonly used to describe such a piece. This one is a copy of an Edmund Townsend blockfront kneehole desk built in Newport, R.I., between 1765 and 1775. The original is now in the Museum of Fine Arts in Boston.

Much of the difficulty in making this reproduction lay in the drawing. The desk is small but quite complex, and I wanted to leave nothing to chance. With the help of the furniture conservation lab at the Museum of Fine Arts and my teachers at the North Bennet Street School, I pulled together the information I needed and made a comprehensive set of full-scale drawings before I cut the first piece of wood. In addition to direct measurements supplied by the museum, I obtained dimensions for parts such as drawers, dividers, and moldings by scaling them from photographs. For other details I relied on writings

NOT A KNEEHOLE, REALLY. You weren't meant to sit down at a small kneehole desk; it was generally used as a bureau.

about Townsend furniture. I found myself trying to take all these bits and pieces of information, some of them based on guesswork, and make them all fit together, hoping to achieve the harmonious proportion I saw in the original.

After 10 days of drafting, using nearly equal amounts of graphite and eraser, I completed a full-scale drawing. From there it was a matter of applying basic cabinetmaking skills and six months of concentrated effort.

ANDREW McINNES

Maple Tavern Table

COLONIAL GEOMETRY. An oval top on a rectangular base and a mix of turned and square parts give this 18th-century reproduction its poise.

A tavern table wasn't always found in a tavern. The term describes a wide range of small, low, easily portable tables with one-board tops and four legs strengthened by stretchers. Although such tables were certainly used in Colonial taverns, the style was adapted to a variety of domestic settings. Smaller ones might have been used for tea service or as occasional tables; larger ones were used for dining.

I found the table on which I based mine in *The New Fine Points of Furniture*, the revised edition of Albert Sack's classic book known to many by its nickname: *Good, Better, Best.* The original table, built in Rhode Island between about 1700 and 1730, appealed to my taste for the elegant yet utilitarian. I liked its compact size and its proportions, and I found the splay of the legs and their fine turnings to be stately. I was also drawn to the simple geometry of an oval top with a rectangular frame below.

I built with curly maple to enliven the surfaces of the table. This was in the spirit of the original, which had a painted surface. Under a clear finish the silver shimmer of the curly maple's reversing grain is exciting but doesn't compete with the overall geometry of the piece or with the modeling of its turned parts.

I'm pleased with the way the table came out, but that merely reminds me of what Albert Sack said when I met him and praised his new book: "It's only a start."

UNCOMMON CANT. Legs canted in two directions were unusual on Colonial tavern tables. Introducing even a slight rake can produce a more refined design.

SPECIFICATIONS

- DIMENSIONS
  28¾ in. long, 20 in. wide, and
  24¾ in. high.

- MATERIALS
  Curly maple.

- FINISH
  Shellac and thinned polyurethane
  varnish.

JONATHAN McLEAN

Reproduction Bombé Desk

SLANT TOP OVER A SWELLED FRONT. This reproduction of an 18th-century Massachusetts desk with a serpentine front was altered from the original to lower the writing surface height.

As a professional furniture maker, I might wait my entire life for that perfect commission. In the meantime, I try to build one or two pieces a year that I wouldn't mind keeping—even though they will always be for sale. The bombé desk is one of these.

My inspiration for this desk came from a picture in a furniture book. Although the maker was not known, the desk was referred to as the Brinley desk (circa 1770) because of an inscription on one of the lopers suggesting that it belonged to Edward Brinley of Weston, Mass. The piece now resides in the Winterthur Museum in Delaware and is considered to be one of the most highly developed examples of the bombé form. Of the more than 50 original bombé desks that still exist, all were made in or around Boston.

Given that this piece is one of the most complicated I could undertake, a full-scale drawing was appropriate. After scaling the photograph and looking at some other examples of slant-front desks, I decided to make some changes. First, I found that most of the writing surfaces were about 34 in. high and I wanted to lower that if at all possible. I eventually reduced the height of the feet to get the writing surface down to 32⅜ inches.

SPECIFICATIONS

■ **DIMENSIONS**
37½ in. long, 20 in. wide, and 43½ in. high.

■ **MATERIALS**
Mahogany, poplar, and brass.

■ **FINISH**
French polish over linseed oil.

The next consideration was the lumber. I found a great piece of 12/4 mahogany for the sides and drawer fronts. It was 29 in. wide and more than 9 ft. long. This helped determine the dimensions of the desk. It ended up being about an inch narrower than the Brinley desk. I also chose to have the center of the drawers protrude ¼ inch farther than the sides. These two changes accentuated the serpentine shape of this reproduction bombé desk.

CURVES INSIDE CURVES. Behind the slant top of this bombé desk, very careful use of the figure in the grain—both horizontal and vertical—accentuates the curves of the inside drawers and the details of the desk's pigeonholes.

CHRIS ARATO has been making and restoring 18th-century furniture for 25 years. Along with Lou Irion, he founded Irion Co. Furnituremakers in 1978. He continues to make high-quality furniture for Irion Co. in Christana, PA from his one-man shop in northern Maine.

G.R. CLIDENCE owns 18th Century Woodworks, a company that focuses on the restoration and reproduction of historic mill sites, waterwheels and related machinery, traditional buildings, and period beds and tables from a shop in West Kingston, RI.

LES CIZEK left his day job in 1986 to pursue woodworking full-time. His work has been featured in the books *Treasure Chests* (The Taunton Press 2001) and *With Wakened Hands: Furniture by James Krenov and Students* (Cambium Press 2000). He recently opened a new shop in Ft. Bragg, FL.

CARL CLINTON has been a woodworker for 25 years. He teaches woodworking as a continuing education course and conducts lectures and demonstrations on woodworking.

SAM FLETCHER has been making furniture and tools for 56 years. He lives in Mechanicsville, VA.

JEFFREY P. GREENE specializes in replicating Newport Goddard and Townsend furniture and is the exclusive replicator of these pieces for the Newport Historical Society, Rhode Island Historical Society, and the Newport Restoration Foundation. He is also the author of *American Furniture in the 18th Century* (The Taunton Press 1996).

EMYL JENKINS is a senior member of the American Society of Appraisers and is the author of *Emyl Jenkins' Reproduction Furniture: Antiques for the Next Generation* (Crown, 1995).

JEFF JUSTIS, JR. is a retired surgeon who has been working wood for over 50 years. In addition to reproducing American furniture from the 18th and 19th centuries, he also builds and pilots small airplanes.

JEFFERSON KOLLE has been fiddling around with wood in one form or another since he got a Tiny Tots set at age three. He is currently working as an editor for *This Old House* magazine.

STEVE LATTA teaches woodworking at the Thaddeus Stevens College of Technology in Lancaster, PA while also pursuing a masters degree in American Studies at Penn State University. He serves on the executive board of the Society of American Period Furnituremakers.

WILLIAM E. LOCKE has spent the last 25 years working with wood—building homes, working in architectural millwork shops and making period and studio furniture. From his shop in West Roxbury, MA, he installs custom architectural millwork and makes custom furniture.

PHILIP LOWE taught woodworking for 10 years at the North Bennett Street School. Since 1985 he has operated a furniture making and restoration shop in Beverly, MA for homes and museums throughout North America.

ROBERT MCCULLOUGH carves full-time in his one-man shop west of Philadelphia. After studying figurative sculpture at Westchester University, he worked at Irion Company Furnituremakers. Now, on his own, he continues to work for Irion and other period furniture makers.

ANDREW MCINNES studied furniture making at the North Bennet Street School. He now manages the wood shop at the Boston Architectural Center.

JONATHAN MCLEAN has been woodworking for over 25 years. He received the 1994 American Woodworker Excellence in Craftsmanship Award in the professional category.

DOUG MOOBERRY started Kinloch Woodworking, Ltd. in 1982. This 18th century furniture shop has grown into a nine-person company with 70,000 board feet of a large variety of woods from which to choose.

RANDALL O'DONNELL began working with wood by building houses, kitchens, architectural millwork, and then furniture. His interest in furniture evolved into a passion for Early American furniture. He also lectures, demonstrates, and hosts workshops in his studio in Indiana.

LANCE PATTERSON is an instructor in the cabinet and furniture making course at the North Bennet Street School in Boston, MA.

JENNIFER A. PERRY is a graduate of the Winterthur Museum Master of Arts program in Early American Culture. She is the education curator at the Florence Griswold Museum in Old Lyme, CT.

WALTER RAYNES divides his time between building custom furniture and restoring European and American antiques for private collectors and museums. He lives and works in Baltimore, MD.

ROBERT TREANOR is a cabinetmaker and teacher in San Francisco.

PETER VAN BECKUM trained at the North Bennett Street School in Boston, MA. He creates custom made reproduction furniture from his shop in Connecticut.

JOHN VAN BUREN is a retired neurosurgeon. He has spent much of the last 30 years building furniture for his family.

NORMA WATKINS is a professional writer who lives in Florida.

ROB WIGGENHORN is a civil engineer for Boeing Aircraft. He started woodworking in 1989 and intends to turn his hobby into a part-time business. He lives in Everett, Washington.

PAUL ZENATY designs and builds custom furniture from his shop in Vermont where he is also an active member of the Vermont Wood Net and Vermont Furnituremakers Guild. His work was included in the *Custom Furniture Sourcebook* (The Taunton Press 2001).

CREDITS

The articles compiled in this book appeared in the following issues of *Fine Woodworking* (FWW) or *Home Furniture* (HF).

p. 6: Federal Furniture Was Revolutionary by Jennifer A. Perry, *HF* issue 11. Photos by Jefferson Kolle, © The Taunton Press, Inc. Photos on pp. 7, 11, 12, 13 taken at Strawbery Banke Museum, Portsmouth, NH; pp. 8–9 at David Dunton Antiques, Woodbury Conn.

P. 14: Queen Anne by Emyl Jenkins, *HF* issue 5. Photos on pp. 15, 16, 17 (top), 18 (bottom), 20 (center) courtesy of Christie's New York; pp. 17 (bottom), 19 courtesy of Chipstone Foundation; pp. 18 (top), 21 (left, center) courtesy of Winterthur Museum; p. 20 (left) courtesy of Collection of Museum of Early Southern Decorative Arts; p. 20 (right) courtesy of Wilton House Museum, Richmond, VA; p. 21 (right) © Dirk Bakker.

p. 22: Choosing Brass Hardware for Period Furniture by Walter Raynes, *HF* issue 2. Photos on pp. 22, 23, 25 by Zachary Gaulkin, © The Taunton Press, Inc.; p. 27 by Susan Kahn, © The Taunton Press, Inc. Hardware courtesy of Ball and Ball and Horton Brasses.

p. 28: The Chippendale Style by Emyl Jenkins, *HF* issue 8. Photo on p. 29 courtesy of Christies of New York; pp. 30, 35 courtesy of Neal Auction Co., New Orleans, La.; pp. 31–33 courtesy of Sotheby's © 2002; p. 33 (left) courtesy of William Doyle Galleries, New York, NY; p. 34 courtesy of The Metropolitan Museum of Art, John Stewart Kennedy Fund, 1918. Photograph by Richard Creek. Photograph © 1985 The Metropolitan Museum of Art.

p. 36: The Age of Mahogany by Les Cizek and Norma Watkins, *HF* issue 14. Photos pp. 36, 37, 42, 43 by Tim Schreiner, © The Taunton Press, Inc.; p. 38 courtesy of Thompson Mahogany, Philadelphia; p. 39 (top) reprinted from Mahogany, Antique, and Modern (1926); (bottom) Metropolitan Museum of Art; p. 40 courtesy of The Herbarium of Fairchild Tropical Garden, Miami; p. 41 courtesy of Collection of the Museum of Early Southern Decorative Arts. Map on p. 37 by Jennifer Thermes.

p. 46: Making Ogee Bracket Feet by Sam Fletcher, *FWW* issue 119. Photos on p. 46 by Scott Phillips, © The Taunton Press, Inc. pp. 47–51 Dennis Preston, © The Taunton Press, Inc.

p. 52: Drop-Leaf Breakfast Table by Robert Treanor, *FWW* issue 104. Photos by Jonathan Binzen, © The Taunton Press, Inc. Illustration by Lee Hov, © The Taunton Press, Inc.

p. 59: Making a Sheraton Bed by Philip C. Lowe, *FWW* issue 113. Photos by Charley Robinson. Illustrations by Kathleen Rushton, © The Taunton Press, Inc.

p. 66: Veneering an Ellipse by John M. Van Buren, *FWW* issue 124. Photos by William Duckworth, © The Taunton Press, Inc.

p. 69: Oval Chippendale Stool by Randall O'Donnell, *FWW* issue 135. Photos on p. 69 (top), 72 (right top and bottom), 73 (top), 75 (center, bottom left), 76 by Dennis Preston © The Taunton Press; pp. 69 (bottom), 72 (left), 73 (bottom), 74, 75 (top and right), 77 Michael Pekovich, © The Taunton Press, Inc. Illustrations by Bob La Pointe, © The Taunton Press, Inc.

p. 78: Pembroke Table by Jefferson Kolle, *FWW* issue 138. Photos by Michael Pekovich, © The Taunton Press, Inc. Illustrations by Bob La Pointe, © The Taunton Press, Inc.

p. 88: Federal-Style Oval Inlays by Steve Latta, *FWW* issue 138. Photos by Anatole Burkin, © The Taunton Press, Inc. Illustrations by Vince Babak, © The Taunton Press, Inc.

p. 98: Curly Cherry Highboy (Part I) by Randall O'Donnell, *FWW* issue 117. Photos on p. 98 by Boyd Hagen, © The Taunton Press, Inc.; pp. 100–105 by Dennis Preston, © The Taunton Press, Inc. Illustrations by Bob La Pointe, © The Taunton Press, Inc.

p. 106: Curly Cherry Highboy (Part II) by Randall O'Donnell, *FWW* issue 118. Photos on pp. 107–115 by Dennis Preston, © The Taunton Press, Inc.; p. 107 inset) by Boyd Hagen, © The Taunton Press, Inc. Illustrations by Bob La Pointe, © The Taunton Press, Inc.

p. 116: Curly Cherry Highboy (Part III) by Randall O'Donnell, *FWW* issue 119. Photos by Dennis Preston, © The Taunton Press, Inc. Illustrations by Bob La Pointe, © The Taunton Press, Inc.

p. 128: Salem Secretary in Figured Mahogany by Doug Mooberry and Kevin Arnold, *HF* issue 7. Photos © Bill Deering.

p. 132: 18th-Century Card Table by Walter Raynes and Carl Clinton, *HF* issue 6. Photos © Joel Breger and Associates.

p. 134: A Desk with Distinguished Ancestry by Jeffrey P. Greene, *HF* issue 3. Photos by Zachary Gaulkin, © The Taunton Press, Inc.

p. 138: Chippendale Dining Chairs by Rob Wiggenhorn, *HF* issue 1. Photos © Rob Wiggenhorn. Illustration © Michael Gellatly.

p. 142: Curly Maple Secretary by Paul Zenaty, *HF* issue 1. Photos © Paul Zenaty. Illustrations © Paul Zenaty.

p. 145: Philadelphia Highboy by Chris Arato and Robert McCullough, *HF* issue 3. Photos by Jonathan Binzen, © The Taunton Press, Inc.

p. 148: Sheraton Field Bed by G.R. Clidence, *HF* issue 3. Photos by Zachary Gaulkin, © The Taunton Press, Inc.

p. 152: Mahogany Federal Sideboard by Lance Patterson, *HF* issue 6. Photos © Lance Patterson.

p. 156: Queen Anne Hall Table by E. Jeff Justis, Jr., *HF* issue 2. Photos by Zachary Gaulkin, © The Taunton Press, Inc. Illustration © Bob La Pointe.

p. 158: Sheraton Armchair by Peter Van Beckum, *HF* issue 6. Photos by Jonathan Binzen, © The Taunton Press, Inc.

p. 160: Townsend Kneehole Desk by William E. Locke, *HF* issue 9. Photos © Lance Patterson.

p. 162: Maple Tavern Table by Andrew McInnes, *HF* issue 9. Photos by Jonathan Binzen, © The Taunton Press, Inc.

p. 164: Reproduction Bombé Desk by Jonathan McLean, *HF* issue 9. Photos © Lance Patterson.

Front matter photo credits

p. ii: Jefferson Kolle, © The Taunton Press, Inc. (left); © Bill Deering (center); Anatole Burkin, © The Taunton Press, Inc. (right).

p. iii: Zachary Gaulkin, © The Taunton Press, Inc.

p. vi: Zachary Gaulkin, © The Taunton Press, Inc.

p. 1: Charley Robinson, © The Taunton Press, Inc. (top left); Jonathan Binzen, © The Taunton Press, Inc. (top right); Michael Pekovich, © The Taunton Press, Inc. (bottom).

p. 2: © Lance Patterson.

Section openers photo credits

p. 4: Zachary Gaulkin, © The Taunton Press, Inc. (left); Jefferson Kolle at David Dunton Antiques, Woodbury, Conn., © The Taunton Press, Inc. (center and right).

p. 5: Jefferson Kolle at Strawbery Banke Museum, © The Taunton Press, Inc.

p. 44: Dennis Preston, © The Taunton Press, Inc.

p. 45: Anatole Burkin, © The Taunton Press, Inc.

p. 126: Jonathan Binzen, © The Taunton Press, Inc. (left); © Joel Breger and Associates (center); Zachary Gaulkin, © The Taunton Press, Inc.

p. 127: Jonathan Binzen, © The Taunton Press, Inc.